Greene and Kierkegaard
The Discourse of Belief

Greene and

Kierkegaard
The Discourse of Belief
Anne T. Salvatore

The University of Alabama Press

Tuscaloosa and London

Copyright © 1988 by
The University of Alabama Press
Tuscaloosa, Alabama 35487
All rights reserved
Manufactured in the United States of America

Library of Congress Cataloging-in-Publication Data

Salvatore, Anne T., 1941–
  Greene and Kierkegaard : the discourse of belief.

  Bibliography: p.
  Includes index.
  1. Greene, Graham, 1904–   —Religion.
  2. Kierkegaard, Søren, 1813–1855—Influence.   3. Belief and doubt in literature.   I. Title.
  PR6013.R44Z83   1988   823'.912   86-19279
  ISBN 0-8173-0332-4

British Library Cataloguing in Publication data is available.

For Nick, Scott, Kevin, and
Kristin — one small
work of love

Contents

	Acknowledgments	ix
	Preface	xiii
1.	Form, Standpoint, and Existential Possibility	1
2.	Author, Narrator, and Reader: The Art of Communicating	18
3.	The Force of Ambiguity: Politics and the Individual	44
4.	Toward an Actual Self: A Theory of Characterization	67
	Conclusion	106
	Notes	108
	Works Cited	113
	Index	120

Acknowledgments

To Mr. Graham Greene, who graciously answered my letters and, in doing so, helped substantiate the thesis of this book, I express sincere gratitude. With deepest appreciation, too, I thank Temple University professors Charles Burkhart, Daniel O'Hara, and Alan Wilde, whose commentary on the manuscript in its original form helped me to crystallize my goals and synthesize the issues; I benefited not only from their wisdom but also from the warm and friendly manner of their support. I am grateful for the kind, always pleasant, editorial assistance of Craig Noll and of Judith Knight and the staff of The University of Alabama Press. My husband, Nick, my parents, Anthony and Mary De Stefano, and friends Marybeth Leary and Phyllis Wachter provided the optimism and long-term encouragement that helped me finish the task. Finally, I am indebted to the Holy Ghost, who represents for me, as for Monsignor Quixote, a "full bottle of wine" and who, I believe, must have been active in the preparation of this book.

An earlier version of one chapter of this book first appeared in *College Literature* 12:1 (1985): 26–32, under the title "Socratic Midwifery: Greene and Kierkegaard." Copyright 1985, West Chester University.

Acknowledgments

I would like to thank the following publishers and individuals for permission to quote from the materials listed:

Graham Greene and Elizabeth Dennys: From a personal letter from Graham Greene, dated March 28, 1984.

Harper & Row, Publishers, Inc.: From *The Concept of Irony* by Søren Kierkegaard. Translated by Lee M. Capel. English translation copyright © 1965 by William Collins Sons & Co., Ltd., London, and Harper & Row, Publishers, Inc., New York. Reprinted by permission of Harper & Row. From *The Point of View for My Work as an Author* by Søren Kierkegaard. Translated by Walter Lowrie. Copyright © 1962 by Harper & Row, Publishers, Inc. Reprinted by permission of Harper & Row.

Indiana University Press: From *Journals and Papers*, volumes 1–4, by Søren Kierkegaard. Edited and translated by Howard V. Hong and Edna H. Hong, assisted by Gregor Malantschuk. Copyright 1967, 1970, 1975, 1975.

Laurence Pollinger Ltd.: From *A Burnt-out Case* by Graham Greene. Copyright © 1960, 1961 by Graham Greene. From *The Comedians* by Graham Greene. Copyright © 1965, 1966 by Graham Greene. From *The End of the Affair* by Graham Greene. Copyright © 1951, 1979 by Graham Greene. From *The Heart of the Matter* by Graham Greene. Copyright © 1948, 1976 by Graham Greene. From *The Honorary Consul* by Graham Greene. Copyright © 1973 by Graham Greene. From *The Quiet American* by Graham Greene. Copyright © 1955, 1983 by Graham Greene. From *Ways of Escape* by Graham Greene. Copyright © 1980 by Graham Greene.

Lester & Orpen Dennys: From *Ways of Escape* by Graham Greene. Copyright © 1980 by Graham Greene. Published in Canada by Lester & Orpen Dennys Ltd., Toronto.

Princeton University Press: From *Attack upon "Christendom"* by Søren Kierkegaard. Translated by Walter Lowrie. Copyright 1944, © renewed by Princeton University Press. From *Concluding Unscientific Postscript* by Søren Kierkegaard. Translated by David F. Swenson and Walter Lowrie. Copyright 1941, © 1969 renewed by

Acknowledgments

Princeton University Press. From *Either/Or* by Søren Kierkegaard. Translated by David F. Swenson and Lillian Marvin Swenson. Copyright 1944, © 1972 renewed by Howard A. Johnson. From *The Sickness unto Death* in *Fear and Trembling* and *The Sickness unto Death* by Søren Kierkegaard. Translated with Introductions and Notes by Walter Lowrie. Copyright 1941, 1954, © 1982 renewed by Princeton University Press.

Simon & Schuster: From *Ways of Escape* by Graham Greene. Copyright © 1980 by Graham Greene. Used by Permission of Simon & Schuster. From *The Honorary Consul* by Graham Greene. Copyright © 1973 by Graham Greene.

Viking Penguin, Inc.: From *A Burnt-out Case* by Graham Greene. Copyright © 1960, 1961 by Graham Greene. From *The Comedians* by Graham Greene. Copyright © 1965, 1966 by Graham Greene. From *The End of the Affair* by Graham Greene. Copyright © 1951, renewed © 1979 by Graham Greene. From *The Heart of the Matter* by Graham Greene. Copyright 1948, renewed © 1976 by Graham Greene. From *The Quiet American* by Graham Greene. Copyright 1955, renewed © 1983 by Graham Greene.

William Collins Sons & Co., Ltd.: From *The Concept of Irony* by Søren Kierkegaard. Translated by Lee M. Capel. Copyright © 1965. Used by permission.

Preface

With the rising importance of the antinovel, together with the striking innovation and the relative opacity that often accompany it, many current writers of traditional, more conventional, and generally more readable fiction have seemed to be anachronisms. The search for meaning in a text, too, has lost much of its previous appeal, at least with those readers and critics who, after being schooled on the ideas of theoreticians such as Ferdinand de Saussure and Jacques Derrida, expect to find no meaning beyond language itself, either in the text or, often, in the world. In this context, a writer whose expressed ideology implies a reality beyond language might well be considered an anomaly.

If one were to consider Graham Greene in such a position (as some scholars have done), one would also have to account for his continued success, both as an artistic manipulator of the fictional process and as an entertainer in the popular field. The latter accomplishment is easier to explain. The exciting plots, the generally simple style, and the politically intriguing subjects of his novels tend to democratize his appeal. Because so much of his fiction deals with religious, often specifically Roman Catholic, topics or characters, he seems to invite a sometimes blind allegiance from the religious segment of the population as well, many of whom view him (I think erroneously) as a stalwart upholder of official church doctrine.

How, then, has he been able to make his mark among many academicians—literary scholars who include his works among their investigations or who teach his novels in their courses? Or more specifically, how should Greene's literary position be defined and evaluated in the context of serious fiction, both traditional and contemporary? This question is the central one in this book. I also consider whether or how Greene could, through the fictional process, be adopting an apparently negative standpoint to make an ultimately positive statement, or whether, even, he is making any statement at all.

To accomplish these objectives and to place some of Greene's major novels in the most illuminating position I could find, I have chosen to explore an analogue of his work—the writings of Søren Kierkegaard. The pairing creates an odd couple at first glance: Greene, born in 1904, a Britisher who lives and writes in France in the tumultuous twentieth century, who has experienced two world wars, who has traveled widely to exotic, often chaotic, places, and who maintains diverse contacts; and Kierkegaard (1813–55), a Dane who lived during an apparently more conservative century, led a relatively parochial life with few friends and even fewer travels, and died a premature death at the age of forty-two; Greene, whose novels with their facile readability are often best-sellers and, almost immediately upon their publication, are translated into a dozen or so other languages; Kierkegaard, whose involuted, abstract, esoteric style has almost completely separated him from the popular audience and, until recently, from most other nations and cultures as well; Greene, the converted "Roman Catholic atheist"; Kierkegaard, the confirmed Lutheran; Greene, regarded as a rationalist; Kierkegaard, branded as an intuitionist; Greene, the apparent representative of church officialdom; Kierkegaard, in seeming opposition to the church establishment; and, of course, Greene, primarily a novelist, versus Kierkegaard, insistently a philosopher/theologian.

Yet, despite these apparent differences, Greene has asserted in personal correspondence that he is "a great admirer of Kierkegaard." And indeed, both artists seem to struggle with the same broadly Christian moral and religious issues; both, I argue, show concern for the implications of the creative process. In addition, each manifests a strikingly similar philosophical view of irony, and each applies this view in dialectical, fictional structures. Moreover, the two writers probe similar covert methods of eliciting response from their readers, even while they stand in the delicate arena of political questions; furthermore, both authors view their characters mimetically as spiritually real selves in a finite world of division and chaos.

But perhaps most important, I hope to demonstrate that Kierkegaard and Greene create with their art a metaphor of belief—usually in a Transcendental Reality, in the possibility of an integral relationship with that Reality, and in the necessity of applying that relationship to every facet of human existence, including, apparently, the act of creating fictional discourse. I use "discourse" in its broadest sense: it is all parts or any one part of the "dynamic system of communicational instructors with a variable meaning-potential which is defined by specifying co-texts and contexts" (Schmidt 1975, 401).

In my selection of Greene's novels to discuss at length, I have striven not so much to be comprehensive (an impossible task for a writer so prolific) as to be representative, both of differing methods and of various periods in Greene's long career. In general, I have selected only from what I consider novels of major importance in his canon. Undoubtedly, some readers will disagree with me on the criteria one should use to judge a novel as "major" or "minor," if indeed one should presume to make such a judgment at all. Greene himself, in fact, has in recent years decided to drop the distinguishing label "entertainment" that he previously used for some of his books; all are now listed as "novels" in the Collected Edition. Yet, I believe one can still distinguish between the two types for purposes of literary criticism. In the minor works, plot seems to dominate, and moral, religious, or artistic questions, while often present, tend to recede in importance as the reader's attention generally becomes focused more superficially on *what* is happening rather than on *why* it is happening; situation, in other words, takes precedence over perplexing subtleties of motivation or self-development. Furthermore, a pattern of suspense and then relief leads to a fairly satisfying, easily achieved catharsis for the reader, who can avoid involvement with the complicated issues raised by the more intricate dramas in the major novels.

In *A Gun for Sale*, for example, a reader's tension may be easily relieved through the "happily ever after" ending because such tension has been predicated mainly on the *situation* of the characters' physical or emotional survival. In contrast, *Brighton Rock*, emphasizing causes and effects of the situation and exploring in much more depth the characters' effort or lack of effort toward ethical/spiritual self-development, continues its dilemma even on the final pages, forcing readers to debate questions which loom far more threateningly before us and which carry the most profound ethical, religious, and, at times, artistic implications. Though an astute reader may detect essential questions in either type of novel, the minor novels contain fewer issues to ponder.

The Human Factor is another example of a novel in which Greene hints at a moral/religious question, in this case the discrepancy between the abstract nature of a concept and the concrete consequences of it, but here too he emphasizes the outcome less than the question itself. The same issue, but with many more of its torturing complexities, is dramatized convincingly in *The Quiet American*; hence, I have chosen the latter as a more useful illustration of this particular Kierkegaardian idea. While many of the early books (such as *The Man Within*, *The Confidential Agent*, *The Ministry of Fear*, and *The Third Man*) have not been chosen for a similar reason, some (*The Power and the Glory*, for instance) might also have been included, since they do meet the criteria for major works. I have omitted such novels only because another one in some way seems to offer a closer parallel with the Kierkegaardian spirit or with the particular tenet I am attempting to illustrate.

From Kierkegaard's equally overwhelming body of work, I have chosen those writings which coincide most, in methodology or in philosophy, with the issues raised by Greene. The works selected span the chronology of his canon and include the "aesthetic" books, the "edifying" discourse, and many of his journal commentaries in which he explores the issues directly.

I use English translations of Kierkegaard's works, quoting generally from editions that are commonly available. For Greene, I have used, whenever possible, the Collected Edition (still in the process of publication by Heinemann and the Bodley Head), which includes, for each volume, a new introduction by the author and his latest, though generally minor, textual revisions.

Greene and Kierkegaard
The Discourse of Belief

1

Form, Standpoint, and Existential Possibility

In his introduction to *Writing Degree Zero*, Roland Barthes comments:

> We shall see . . . that the ideological unity of the bourgeoisie gave rise to a single mode of writing, and that in the bourgeois periods (classical and romantic), literary form could not be divided because consciousness was not; whereas, as soon as the writer ceased to be a witness to the universal, to become the incarnation of a tragic awareness (around 1850), his first gesture was to choose the commitment of his form, either by adopting or rejecting the writing of his past. ([1953] 1967, 2–3)

In one sense, Graham Greene seems to have adopted the writing of his past. His instructor in technique, by his own admission, was Percy Lubbock, whose 1921 publication became the theoretical bible for many writers of traditional fiction. Greene notes in his first autobiography: "My long studies in Percy Lubbock's *The Craft of Fiction* had taught me the importance of 'the point of view'" (1971, 202–3). In addition, the literary ancestors Greene reveres tend to be craftsmen of the "art" novel, such as Joseph Conrad, Ford Madox Ford, and Henry James. Although Greene later came to believe he had outgrown some of Conrad's techniques, particularly the inflated use of language, he nevertheless acknowledges his debt to his predecessor, noting, for example, "how often he compares something concrete to something abstract. Is it a trick I have caught?" (1962, 33). The use of depth psychology, apparent in the characterizations of Marlow and Kurtz in Conrad's *Heart of Darkness*, is another technique prevalent in the Flaubertian form of the art novel; Greene adopts the method as both structure and theme in *A Burnt-Out Case*.

Ford Madox Ford is a second novelist who demonstrates a traditionalist attention to form. As John A. Meixner points out, Ford belonged to the school of writing which stresses "the careful, suggestive, economic selection of incident and detail—and which strives to approximate the aesthetic rigor and formal shapeliness associated with poetry and the drama" (1962, 5). Commenting on *The Good Soldier* in a critical essay on Ford, Greene himself gives the novel high praise for its successful technique, describing it as "undoubtedly Ford's masterpiece"; Greene further notes that the book is one of the "novels which stand as high as any fiction written since the death of James" (1969, 165, 161).

Henry James also exerted a major influence on Greene's writing. Referring to the "beautiful symmetry" of the Jamesian form of the novel (1969, 53), Greene clearly has in mind the closed form of the traditional novel that emphasizes unity above all else. As he explains in *A Sort of Life*, he became a novelist because of "a desire to reduce a chaos of experience to some sort of order" (1971, 12)—a remark which sounds quite similar to one made by James, at typically greater length, in the preface to *The Awkward Age*:

> The Thing "done," artistically, is a fusion, or it has not *been* done—in which case of course the artist may be, and all deservedly, pelted with any fragment of his botch the critic shall choose to pick up. But his ground once conquered, in this particular field, he knows nothing of fragments and may say in all security: "Detach one if you can. You can analyze in *your* way, oh yes—to relate, to report, to explain; but you can't disintegrate my synthesis; you can't resolve the elements of my whole into different responsible agents." (1908, xxii)

Like Henry James's novels, Greene's fictions are masterpieces of fusion, with each element of the artist's technique meshing into a wholeness through a repeated emphasis on the same theme. The typically linear plot structure, the psychological characterization, the patterns of images woven into symbolic settings, and the use of rhetorical devices linking the concrete with the abstract are technical devices present in Greene's major novels, from *Brighton Rock* (1938) to *Monsignor Quixote* (1982), which combine to reveal the author's belief in human value and purpose—the same beliefs that one can find submerged in the conventional techniques of Greene's literary ancestors.

Yet strangely, his philosophical orientation often appears to be much more contemporary, if not so clearly in some of his earlier books, such as *The Power and the Glory* (1940), in which the redemptive possibility lingers in spite of life's dreariness, then certainly in most of his middle and later novels, such as *The Quiet American* (1955), *A Burnt-Out Case* (1961), *The Comedians* (1966), *Travels with My Aunt* (1970), *Doctor Fischer of Geneva or the Bomb Party* (1980). As many of Greene's nonsectarian critics have noticed, these books seem to emphasize "the terrible calamity in which 'the human race is implicated'" and to display Greene's vision as "savagely pessimistic" (Webster 1963, 3, 9).[1]

Indeed, the books themselves generally confirm Webster's impression. In *Graham Greene: A Critical Essay*, Martin Turnell explains how setting, for example, symbolically represents Greene's vision of horror:

> The Mexico of *The Power and the Glory* and the Gold Coast of *The Heart of the Matter* are as much "a region of the mind" as the Congo of *A Burnt-Out Case*. It is a grim, depressing, suffocating region . . . dead and deadening, a region that drains all hope from life . . . a region which appears somehow to provoke terrifying events. (1967, 18)

The characters, too, add to the reader's impression of futility. From the angry Pinkie in *Brighton Rock* and the despairing Scobie in *The*

Heart of the Matter to the hopeless prisoners of their own illusions, such as Fowler in *The Quiet American*, Brown in *The Comedians*, and Pulling in *Travels with My Aunt*, Greene's fictional representatives of humanity suggest the impossibility of human knowledge; the lack of real freedom; the constant flux, conflict, and ambiguity; and certainly the repeated failure of human beings to achieve, or even become aware of, their own goals.

Greene himself, moreover, apparently agrees with these impressions of his standpoint. In *Ways of Escape*, his most recent autobiography, he chides his critics who think the world should be represented otherwise:

> Some critics have referred to a strange violent "seedy" region of the mind . . . which they call Greeneland, and I have sometimes wondered whether they go round the world blinkered. "This is Indochina," I want to exclaim, "this is Mexico, this is Sierra Leone carefully and accurately described. I have been a newspaper correspondent as well as a novelist. I assure you that the dead child lay in the ditch in just that attitude. In the canal of Phat Diem the bodies stuck out of the water. . . ." But I know that argument is useless. They won't believe the world they haven't noticed is like that. (1980b, 80)

As if to confirm his novelistic stand personally, Greene mentions in his earlier autobiography his attempts to escape the terrible boredom he found in life by risking death through Russian roulette and through "absurd and reckless" treks into war-ravaged lands such as Tabasco, the Kikuyu reserve, Malaya, and Vietnam (1971, 133). For Greene, as for so many other modernist writers (E. M. Forster in his later books, Virginia Woolf, Ford Madox Ford, for example), art is, at least partially, a way of escape: "Writing is a form of therapy; sometimes I wonder how all those who do not write, compose or paint can manage to escape the madness, the melancholia, the panic fear which is inherent in the human situation" (1980b, 285).

To find refuge in the order and symmetry of art, however, is to create an apparently unresolvable, ironic contradiction between the unified formal properties of a novel and its philosophical standpoint, as Alan Wilde suggests (1981, 39–40, 70, 80–81) and as I have been suggesting in my discussion of the tension between Greene's use of the traditional novel form and his stated view of world chaos. In Wilde's consideration of irony not as a formal property but as a philosophical viewpoint, he categorizes this phenomenon as "disjunctive irony," which, he explains, is the "characteristic form of modernism" (p. 10). Distinguishing this type of vision from a less pessimistic type which he calls "mediate" irony and an even more radically pessimistic sort which he terms "suspensive,"[2] Wilde defines disjunctive irony as that which

> strives, however reluctantly, toward a condition of paradox. The ironist, far more basically adrift [than he would be in mediate irony], confronts a world that appears inherently disconnected and fragmented. At its extreme or "absolute" point . . . disjunctive irony both recognizes the disconnections and seeks to control them . . . ; and so the confusions of the world are shaped into an equal poise of opposites: the form of an unresolvable paradox. (P. 10)

The apparent contradiction between Greene's form and his vision would seem to indicate that his novels ought to be described by this category of disjunction. I believe, however, that a somewhat different model of irony exists here, that this model will not fit into any of Wilde's categories as described, and that what is actually being ironized is not only a fragmented human world but, more important, the disjunctive ironic standpoint itself.

To support such a claim, I will consider the classically ironic stance manifested in the theory and art of Søren Kierkegaard. In so doing, I hope to show not that Kierkegaard's vision and methods influenced Greene (although they may have—the latter quotes Kierkegaard in the epigraph to *A Sort of Life*) but that Greene and his nineteenth-century Christian predecessor are kindred spirits and that a study of Kierkegaard's ironic theory and practice therefore illuminates Greene's conscious—and perhaps unconscious—purposes in his use of traditional fictions that conflict with his apparent standpoint.

Like Greene, Kierkegaard seems to view the world negatively, perceiving it as inherently chaotic spiritually, ethically, and psychologically. His journals reveal unmistakably his own standpoint of disillusionment: "the world . . . is little more than scoundrelly" (1967–78, vol. 4, entry 5016); "this world is a world of untruth, of lies, and to live Christianly in it means to suffer" (1:168); "the hypocrisy of the world" (4:5020); "anyone with a little experience knows that it is a trashy world" (4:5025); "the task is really to discover that this world is a vale of tears" (4:5031); "a splendid world, where there is nothing but dishonesty . . . faithlessness . . . where a real man is a wonder which is not only not to be seen but is not even missed . . . everything . . . is a disguise, is not what it pretends to be" (4:5033); "this whole world is like a penitentiary" (4:5037); "this whole matter of history is meaningless" (4:5035).

Like much of Greene's audience, moreover, many of Kierkegaard's readers interpret his standpoint as a negative one. Josiah Thompson's comment in an article on the pseudonymous works is representative:

> What the pseudonyms illustrate is the failure of all attempts to prevent our lives boiling off into the imaginary. Like us, the pseudonyms never succeed in becoming integral, never overcome a fundamental dissipation. . . . What they seek to demonstrate is not the adequacy of a new philosophy, but the nullity of all philosophy. What they seek to exhibit is not the possibilities of a new literary genre, but the final impossibility of all genres. . . . And their repeated and austere comment is that [the imaginative] act must inevitably end in failure. (1972, 162–63)

A similar spirit pervades much of *The Concept of Irony*, Kierkegaard's early academic study of irony as a standpoint, using Socrates' stance as a model and emphasizing the ironist's negative position in relation to actuality. The often-quoted passage in which Kierkegaard uses the "bird's eye" perspective to describe that essentially vertical position is worth repeating here, since the image is so precise a representation of the Socratic standpoint. The ironist

> elevates himself higher and higher, becoming ever lighter as he rises, seeing all things disappear beneath him from his ironical bird's eye perspective, while he himself hovers above them in ironic satisfaction borne by the absolute self-consistency of the infinite negativity within him. Thus he becomes estranged from the whole world to which he belongs (however much he may still belong to it in another sense), the contemporary consciousness affords him no predicates, ineffable and indeterminate he belongs to a different formation. (1968b, 221)

While in context this passage refers to Socrates' relationship to the Greek political state which had condemned him, Kierkegaard surely means also to set up a model of irony which he himself seems to accept as valid; indeed, most of the book tends to confirm this intention through the positive valuation which he continually places upon the Socratic method.

Kierkegaard is accepting, then, infinite absolute negativity, through which the ironist "disdains reality" (1968b, 236) and condemns everything in existence except consciousness, which becomes, in a negative sense at least, free. The Socratic/Kierkegaardian standpoint thus appears initially to resemble Wilde's description of disjunctive irony with its withdrawal from the perception of disconnection and fragmentation. In the very last—and therefore most significant—portion of his dissertation, "Irony as a Mastered Moment," however, Kierkegaard revokes the Socratic position. He asserts here that the artist must seek to control disjunction not only through art ("in the moment of artistic production") but also, and much more important for Kierkegaard, in the artist's own life ("in his own individual existence"). Within the poetic production, Kierkegaard explains, the irony is mastered through a "self-conscious endeavour to order and assign each particular its place in the whole" (p. 337). In the personal life, the author continues, the artist must strive, as Goethe did, to make his existence as a poet agree with his "actuality," or his historical life. When the artist's work and the artist's life have been controlled, then irony has been "mastered" or "reduced to a moment" (p. 377).

To describe Kierkegaard's view of mastered irony, however, is still not to define, totally, his standpoint, for mastering irony does not mean abandoning it. In the same chapter, he indicates that disjunctive irony does have value:

> As philosophers claim that no true philosophy is possible without doubt, so by the same token one may claim that no authentic human life is possible without irony. . . . Irony is a disciplinarian feared only by those who do not know it, but cherished by those who do. He who does not understand irony and has no ear for its whisperings lacks *eo ipso* what might be called the absolute beginning of the personal life. . . . He does not know the invigoration and fortification which, should the atmosphere become too oppressive, comes from lifting oneself up and plunging into the ocean of irony, *not in order to remain there*, but healthily, gladly, lightly to clad oneself again. (1968b, 339; italics mine)

The key words "not in order to remain there" indicate that Kierkegaard's real standpoint is mobile: the artist can and should bathe momentarily in the position of infinite absolute negativity, but only for the purpose of sparking a new and positive beginning for the personal life.[3] After soaring to its high-perched position, therefore, mastered irony becomes horizontal: returning to earth, it "renders finite, defines, and thereby yields truth, actuality, and content." In the shift, negation itself is negated, yet the position does not thereupon become all the more vertical; instead, existence is embraced, yielding, for the first time, truth. For the artist, negativity turns into positivity when existence is thus accepted. In Kierkegaard's words, "The poet only lives poetically when oriented and thus assimilated into the age in which he lives, when he is positively free within the actuality to which he belongs" (1968b, 338).

Obviously, a great leap must take place during this movement, for if existence is perceived by the self as chaotic and fragmented (as it is in *The Concept of Irony*), then how can truth emerge? Has the self merely changed its vision and adopted a naive viewpoint? Does it now assume, as Wilde's mediate ironist does, that the world has only temporarily lapsed from its ethical norm and will eventually be able to correct itself with the proper instruction? Or does the self finally decide to accept the world as permanently fragmented, in a more or less resigned and perhaps humorous way, through an abandonment of the paradise myth, a choice which Wilde's suspensive ironist makes? Or did Kierkegaard, in this early academic work, intend *The Concept of Irony* itself, including the last chapter, to be deeply and profoundly ironic in Wilde's disjunctive sense?

This last objection, if proved, would of course destroy my thesis on Kierkegaard's mobile standpoint and therefore must be dealt with first. It is widely accepted in the criticism of Kierkegaard's works that he consistently opposed the Hegelian system of philosophy, with its emphasis on universals and its resolution of opposites into a higher unity.[4] Hegel, as Kierkegaard himself notes, considered irony to be "an abomination in his sight" (1968b, 282). It seems possible, then, that Kierkegaard deliberately set out to embarrass Hegelians by using the stance of infinite absolute negativity so powerfully that its apparent rebuttal in the last few pages would be seen as intentionally naive. If one had to judge only by *The Concept of Irony*, a decision about meaning in the last chapter would become very difficult, if not impossible. Fortunately, however, Kierkegaard's intention is quite clearly stated in a journal entry written in 1837, four years before he completed his dissertation; the entry indicates in a clear and straightforward manner that Kierkegaard indeed espouses the mobile position he seems to adopt in the chapter on mastered irony: "This self-overcoming of irony is the crisis of the higher spiritual life; the individual is now acclimatized—the bourgeois mentality, which essentially only hides in the other position, is conquered, and the individual is reconciled" (1967–78, 2:1688).[5]

"Irony as a mastered moment," then, can be accepted at face

value. Two questions remain, however. The first, asking whether the self suddenly assumes that the world can be corrected, may be easily dismissed. Kierkegaard's *Journals*, as I demonstrated earlier, show his repeated emphasis on the intrinsically chaotic nature of existence.

The second question is more complicated. While accepting the world, the ironist claims to be embracing truth, even though just denying that truth from the world is possible. The answer, again, lies outside the text of *The Concept of Irony*, this time in *The Point of View for My Work as an Author* and in the *Journals*. In the former, Kierkegaard reveals the kind of truth he accepts; in the latter, he explains the process by which he accepts that truth.

Kierkegaard asserts unambiguously in the introduction to *Point of View*: "The contents of this little book affirm . . . what I truly am as an author, that I am and was a religious author, that the whole of my work as an author is related to Christianity, to the problem 'of becoming a Christian'" (1962a, 5–6). "Truth" for Kierkegaard, then, is religious truth, or Christ. Yet he does not embrace the world in order to find this truth; rather, he finds it first and then embraces the world because of it.

But the locus of the truth presents still another problem, for an artist who transcends self and world (as many religious authors do) in order to find truth has in effect rejected both self and world, has retained negativity, and has not, therefore, in Kierkegaard's sense, "mastered" irony. The *Journals* imply, however, that the locus of truth begins beyond but moves inside of the self; in other words, Christianity emphasizes not the exclusion but the inclusion of the self in the discovery of truth: "To become a single individual, to continue as a single individual, is the way to the truth" (1967–78, 4:4887). Thus, the world may lack truth, or remain fragmented, even while the individual self can attain Christian truth—by choosing to permit a metaphrastic process to occur in which the eternal Idea merges with the temporal self and innovates it: "The union with God . . . takes place in the personality clarified through this whole process" (4:3887). Union is thus allowed by the self, yet the oneness is neither created by the self nor limited to the self. The self, however, is not merely passive, for it has made an active choice; chilled with dread, it has decided to endow itself with meaning and purpose through a Presence that is simultaneously both within and outside of itself. But having chosen, the self finds that its task is far from complete: the individual must realize this Presence in existence; the artist must, in addition, realize it through art. The emphasis on existence here is highly significant, for this existential type of unity differs radically from the rationalistic sort which Hegel proposed and which Kierkegaard vigorously rejected.

Kierkegaard refers to the theory (but not to the application) of this existential process in *The Concept of Irony:* "Irony as a mastered moment exhibits itself in its truth precisely by the fact that it teaches us to actualize actuality, by the fact that it places due emphasis on actuality" (1968b, 340). He does not state explicitly in *The Concept of Irony*, though, that in the production of this new standpoint, consciousness must first accept a belief—not reasoned or even reasonable—in the concept of belief, a "passionate" acceptance of a personal, as opposed to the Hegelian systematic, Idea. In the *Journals*, Kierkegaard calls the process "a leap," "an eternal decision" (1967–78, 3:2354). He emphasizes particularly that only through this leap can one "burst the whole progression of reason and define a qualitative newness"—belief in the eternal Idea (3:2358). He assumes, of course, the referentiality of idea: faith tells him that the personal idea indicates the existence of the eternal Idea, or as his religious works certainly show, he believes—during such periods when he has mastered disjunctive irony—in the reality of a God. Thus, when irony becomes a mastered moment in the individual's life, he or she can begin or recover the movement toward a new "relationship of personality between God and man" (2:1154); through this process, unity can be achieved in addition to and in spite of a worldview of fragmentation.

In this model, mastered irony is both a seducer and a guide. When incorporated into a text, irony beckons the reader to temporary acceptance until, the author hopes, the reader finally awakens to the disastrous results of negativity. In artistic terms, irony should be, then, only a "moment," an existential possibility which can be dramatized by the artist who continually attempts to master it in personal life.[6] In religious terms, as Kierkegaard expresses the principle in his "edifying" works, the individual can and must confront the nihilistic standpoint—but as a springboard to belief in the Idea.

Significant, also, in this model of fragmentation and unity is the change in the direction of the fusion. For Kierkegaard, no longer need the artist seek mediation between existence and idea, or thought. This type of union may be impossible to achieve, since the two spheres, considered only on the human level, are profoundly disjunctive, as the modernists discovered to their own dismay. In Kierkegaard's paradigm, by contrast, the Christian artist achieves a paradoxical unity by merging the self with the Idea (finite with infinite). The artistic project then represents metaphorically the standpoint of real fusion accomplished by the author: purposefully and meaningfully, he or she can, like Professor Heiberg, "assign each particular its place in the whole" (Kierkegaard 1968b, 337). Through the control of form, the artist as Christian consciously expresses a philosophical belief in the achievement, or at least the possibility, of unity, even while faced with persistent fragmentation. When belief is present, then, the discourse is not at odds with the standpoint.

But this belief, it is important to note, differs from the *desire* for unity found in modernist projects (Wilde uses Forster as one example), in which the wish nostalgically persists, but the belief is partially or wholly missing. The inevitable result in such projects is absolute disjunction, for though the appearance of unity lingers, the "art is at odds with" the chaos in the artist's vision (Wilde 1981, 80). Kierkegaard's project also differs from that of some writers in the 1930s, for whom the paradox, as Wilde points out, was more apparent than real. Citing C. Day Lewis's "In Me Two Worlds" and Christopher Isherwood's "Truly Weak Man," Wilde shows that, in these works, the contradictions between thought and existence were actually resolvable. In *The Concept of Irony*, the opposition is both real and persistent; the direction and the subjects of unity undergo the change.

Graham Greene, I suggest, undertakes the same kind of artistic project. Like Kierkegaard's standpoint, Greene's position is mobile: using infinite absolute negativity as an artistic technique, he presents characters who embody the stance. Condemning everything, including God, one another, society, the political state, the church, and even themselves, these characters create the impression of moral and psychological trauma which is frequently accepted as Greene's whole standpoint. If this view of the world were identical with his philosophical standpoint, however, then his use of the traditional novel forms of Conrad, Ford, and James would be merely anachronistic in the context of contemporary fiction. But considered in the light of a Kierkegaardian shifting position, Greene's formal unity becomes a dynamic and continuous statement of philosophical or religious belief in Truth, intentionally exploding the negative standpoint of his fellow modernists and of his characters. The latter thus become not just ironic examples of endless human failures but, more interestingly, the dramatizations of myriad existential moments; indirectly, Greene tries to communicate to his readers what Louis Mackey, in discussing Kierkegaard's works, calls a poetic "insight into [existential] possibilities" (1972, 96).

A few of Greene's critics, in fact, have already detected his existential tendencies in general and his relationship to Kierkegaardian existential thinking in particular. James Noxon, for example, analyzes Greene's method of "dramatizing . . . [the] existential dialectic" in *A Burnt-Out Case* (1962, 100). Noxon is careful to add, of course, that he does not attempt to prove any conscious intent by Greene to dramatize Kierkegaard's "stages" of existence, suggesting only that the novel may be profitably read with the stages in mind. The same novel and subject are treated in Hanlon 1977, which links several different characters in the novel with Kierkegaard's existential possibilities: the aesthetic, the ethical, and the religious. Using a somewhat different emphasis, Lucio P. Ruotolo (1964) analyzes

Brighton Rock and shows how Pinkie negates all types of existence possibilities, thereby fleeing from his own self as well. Sister Marian, finally, although not linking Greene with Kierkegaard, maintains that Greene's characters do exhibit "existential" qualities in "their dawning consciousness of what their being is and what it means *to become*" (1965, 17).

To connect Greene with existentialism, though, is to risk a misunderstanding, for like the term "irony," "existentialism" carries the burden of numerous connotations. The existentialism of Camus and Sartre, for example, in which humankind is viewed as an absurdity in a meaningless universe, has little in common with the existentialism of Kierkegaard and Greene. Perhaps even more confusing is the varying usage of the term in literary criticism as a synonym for almost anything negative. To Gerald Levin, existentialism seems to signify "uncertainty" or "indeterminateness" in *The Heart of the Matter* (1970, 18). Harold Barratt, analyzing the same novel, finds that Scobie is an existentialist because he is a "situationalist" (1965, 328). Andrzej Weselinski, like the first two critics, does not define his term but implies that existentialism indicates hopelessness; he asserts that "Greene's view of Scobie's plight is existential" because "he seems to show little faith in the possibilities of human good" or because "Scobie's actions, despite his best intentions, bring disastrous effects" (1976, 171). Finally, Robert O. Evans (1957) uses "existentialism" to refer to such diverse elements in *The Quiet American* as freedom of choice, amorality, political leftism, and suffering.

Kierkegaard's use of the term is quite different. Unlike Camus and Sartre, for whom existentialism becomes a philosophy, Kierkegaard considers existence to be "the very opposite of system" (Mackey 1969, 38). In a journal entry made in 1850, Kierkegaard implies the primacy of experience over thought and indicates what he considers the most important usage for his version of existentialism: "The portrayal of the existential is chiefly either realization in life or poetic presentation, *loquere ut videam* [speak that I may perceive]" (1967–78, 1:1058; trans. p. 538). Notably absent are the negative implications of much contemporary existentialist theory; projecting a more positive attitude, Kierkegaardian existentialism indicates the way human beings choose and appropriate eternal truth into their own life.

The same ontological and experiential emphases make Greene's novels the "poetic presentation" of the existential. The characters speak so that the reader may perceive and weigh the advantages and disadvantages of many different life categories. Some characters, purporting to be believers in Christianity, nevertheless fail to appropriate it into their lives; others, nonbelievers, paradoxically lead lives that reveal belief; still others have actually lost all belief and are existing in almost total indifference. At the risk of oversimplification, these three possible existence types (among the many others that Greene portrays) may be applied roughly to his early, middle, and later novels.

The whiskey priest of *The Power and the Glory* (1940), for example, preaches Christian faith and conversion, but like the inhabitants of Kierkegaard's Christendom, through a human weakness he fails to incorporate his principles into his own life experience. This error indirectly causes his own death, for his insistence on serving his people even in the worst of dangers has been, he realizes too late, founded on pride instead of on real love. In *The Heart of the Matter* (1948), Scobie clings strangely to his faith by adhering to church rules and refusing communion while in mortal sin, even while he continues in adultery with Helen Rolt; his belief, Greene implies, remains unrealized in his existence: the acceptance of an external church regulation does not indicate acceptance of the Kierkegaardian metaphrastic process of internal realization of Presence.

That this internality beckons becomes increasingly clear during Greene's middle period. In *The End of the Affair* (1951), he presents Maurice Bendrix as the self-deceptive artist who struggles against belief by denying it so often as to reveal his submerged fascination with it. Sarah, by contrast, is one of very few characters in Greene's fiction who, though at first refusing faith, finally admits belief and effects in her existence the Kierkegaardian fusion between internality and externality; as the title indicates, she ends her affair with

Bendrix and lives out the short remainder of her life as her faith dictates. In *A Burnt-Out Case* (1961), a similar process takes place. Querry begins like Bendrix in apparent nonbelief, but unlike the latter, Querry not only leads a Christian life but, at the moment of death, awakens to the possibility of belief, thereby—if ever so briefly—uniting the temporal self with the eternal Idea, dramatizing the one existential possibility which yields reconciliation even in the midst of persistent fragmentation.

In his later years, Greene portrays the opposite possibility. In these books, the reader views the effects of a pervasive nonbelief that ends in an almost total indifference. Here the disjunctive standpoint is at its most extreme. Brown, the narrator of *The Comedians* (1966), exemplifies this completely negative view of life. He has completely withdrawn from satisfying activity and meaningful relationships. His life has no Truth, and he therefore has no self; Greene surrounds him with images of death. A similar character is Henry Pulling in *Travels with My Aunt* (1970). While Pulling resembles his negative predecessor in withdrawing totally from life, he differs from Brown by deceiving himself into thinking he has accepted life; actually, Pulling embraces only the superficial coating of his Aunt Augusta's globe-trotting; Greene implies in the novel that Henry has inherited Brown's disease: his self has long since died or, worse, has perhaps never even been born. In this existential phase, Greene would probably position many contemporary writers of nonrealist fiction; to him they would be ironists without belief and without self, finding pleasure in the phenomenon, perhaps, but lacking the essence beneath it.

One other existential possibility deserves mention because it demonstrates how Greene has returned in a recent novel, *Monsignor Quixote* (1982), to a study of belief. The priest, in fact, is almost a paradigm of the Kierkegaardian standpoint. Appearing, like Don Quixote himself, as alternately mad and sane, the monsignor wills against all odds to accept the "Absurd Paradox" of a unity between the temporal and the eternal; he does so in spite of the divisiveness and evil which continually assert themselves in his life. Existence for him is, as Kierkegaard presents in *Concluding Unscientific Postscript*, an enthusiastic venture into an uncertainty that can be controlled only through what Walter Lowrie in his introduction calls "a fighting certainty" (1968c, xviii).

The mere variety of these types of potential existence suggests that no one of them can be identified finally as Greene's own. His novels, therefore, need not prompt questions about what kind of "distorted" Christianity Greene espouses in his own life. His standpoint, like Kierkegaard's, is a mobile one: Greene's positivity is expressed in the text through the use of the traditional, unified form which "stands resplendent" (Barthes [1953] 1967, 5); the negativity is revealed through Greene's psychological analyses of characters who follow various existential possibilities to their logical conclusions. His method, finally, is to allow readers to judge for themselves among the possibilities.

2

Author, Narrator, and Reader: The Art of Communicating

"It is the basic error of modern times that everywhere people are occupied with the *what* they are to communicate—not with *what communication is*" (Kierkegaard 1967–78, 1:657). When he recorded this observation in 1847, Kierkegaard was anticipating by more than a century a problem that only recently has come to the widespread attention of literary critics. Occupied with finding a hidden "message" in the text of a work of art, many critics tended to overlook the other components in the communication process. Kierkegaard names four of these: the object, the communicator, the receiver, and the communication (1:651). Referring to the first, he distinguishes between communication that conveys an "object" and that which transmits "no 'object.'"[1] The former he considers "direct communication," or transmission of "knowledge"; the latter, "indirect communication," or transposition of "capability" (1:651–53). Discourse in the empirical sciences, for example, conveys knowledge, while all ethical and some religious communication suggests capability. Knowledge can be transmitted directly because the receiver, Kierkegaard assumes, is willing to accept the object; ethical capability, on the other hand, must be communicated indirectly, since, as he explains in *Point of View*, "a direct attack only strengthens a person in his illusion, and at the same time embitters him" (1962a, 25).

To avoid this offense to the recipient, the communicator in the indirect approach adopts a disguise or "deception" (1967–78, 1:22). Should anyone object to such a practice, Kierkegaard further asserts that "one can deceive a person for the truth's sake, and (to recall old Socrates) one can deceive a person into the truth" (1962a, 39). As Raymond Anderson explains in his comprehensive analysis of Kierkegaard's communication theory, disguise for Socrates consisted of a profession of ignorance (1966, 183); Kierkegaard "deceived" in his aesthetic works through the use of irony (1968c, 450), an "aesthetic incognito" (1962a, 39): that is, the works were signed by pseudonymous "authors" who acted out various roles which did not necessarily reflect Kierkegaard's own views. His public pose was also a kind of "incognito," for he avoided at all costs the role of an authority:

> And now as for me, the author, what, according to my opinion, is my relation to the age? Am I perhaps the "Apostle"? Abominable! I have never given occasion for such a judgement. I am a poor insignificant person. Am I then the teacher, the educator? No not that at all; I am he who himself has been educated, or whose authorship expresses what it is to be educated to the point of becoming a Christian. . . . I am not a teacher only a fellow student. (1962a, 75)

The communicator in the indirect process should, then, adopt the maieutic method of Socrates, who "said he could not give birth but could only be a midwife" (1967–78, 1:19). The process, in its positive form, thus becomes one of "luring the ethical out of the individual, because it is *in* the individual" (1:5). When the communicator intends that "the receiver first be cleansed" of any "illusion," the "negative in the maieutic" (1:30) is used. In this form, "to communicate" would mean "a tricking out of," a method of awakening the recipient to his or her illusions. Under both these forms, the object is de-emphasized in the discourse while the self-activity of the recipient is foregrounded. Anderson specifies the several stages of the reader's active role in relation to the text:

> Discourse can be used to help the recipient become conscious of his present values, to become aware of ways in which he may have been

deceiving himself in regard to his real values, to become convinced of the importance of conscious valuation, to overcome the illusion that his values are objectively grounded, to become perplexed and anxious about his values, and to perceive ethical and religious values as possibilities for himself. (1966, 428)

The result of this activity, Kierkegaard hopes, will be the achievement of "inwardness" or "subjectivity," which he holds to be the first goal of the ethical/religious individual: "Subjectivity is the way of deliverance" (1967–78, 4:4555); "subjectivity must be thoroughly and intensively worked through in order to . . . conceive of an eternal decision, of . . . *eternal* salvation" (4:4537). Thus, Kierkegaard establishes a close relationship between the aesthetic act of reading, the establishment of ethical/religious capability, and the achievement of an eternal goal. For the communicator with ethical/religious intentions, he indicates, the link is an essential one.

In the light of recent studies by Wolfgang Iser and other "reader-response" critics, the application of the Kierkegaardian theory of indirect communication to the modern ethical/religious text seems almost inevitable. In *The Act of Reading: A Theory of Aesthetic Response*, Iser, like Kierkegaard (although not mentioning him), emphasizes the role of the recipient and views the text as part of a dialectical function rather than as an object: "The reader and the literary text are partners in a process of communication"; "our prime concern will no longer be the *meaning* of . . . text but its *effect*" (1978, 54). While not all reader-response critics have moral concerns, Iser's theory seems to head in that direction. He notes, for instance, that a text may prompt a reader to reexamine personal norms, to "take a fresh look at the forces which guide and orient him, and which he may hitherto have accepted without question" (p. 74). For the critic, the essential task is to discover how and why the reader was propelled in a particular direction in his or her relationship with the text.

Both Kierkegaard and Iser offer, among other methods, an antithetical arrangement of perspectives in the text as a causal factor in the process. Kierkegaard describes the method and its rationale in *Point of View:* "The indirect method . . . loving and serving the truth, arranges everything dialectically for the prospective captive, and then shyly withdraws (for love is always shy), so as not to witness the admission which he makes to himself alone before God—that he has lived hitherto in an illusion" (1962a, 25–26). Iser somewhat more comprehensively delineates the same technique, though without the religious element.

> The oppositional arrangement of perspectives . . . sets norms against one another by showing up the deficiencies of each norm when viewed from the standpoint of the others. . . . The context is a product of switching perspectives, and the producer is the reader himself, who removes the norms from their pragmatic setting and begins to see them for what they are, thus becoming aware of the functions they perform in the system from which they have been removed. This is tantamount to saying that he begins to understand the influence the norms have on him in real life. (1978, 101)

The key words here for textual application are "the oppositional arrangement of perspectives," or in Kierkegaardian terminology, the dialectical formation of the text. Hermann Diem defines the strategy as a movement "between . . . assertion and contradiction in dialogue" (1959, 9).[2]

Among Kierkegaard's aesthetic works, *Either/Or* is probably the most striking example of this form. Published in 1840 and the first of his pseudonymous works, the two-volume opus is an imaginative rendering of two opposing existential possibilities, which Kierkegaard calls the "aesthetic" and the "ethical" ways of life. The first of the volumes, *Either,* opens with an account by the purported editor, Victor Eremita, of how he became obsessed with a certain desk, or "secretary," and, after purchasing it at great cost, discovered in it the papers of A and B, which, he tells us, he has decided to publish and which may or may not actually have been written by the same person. Most of this first volume consists of A's writings, with the exception of the "Diary of the Seducer," which A claims he edited but did not write. With this Chinese-box method of enclosing narrative within narrative, Kierkegaard preserves his distance from the readers, who are left to experience for themselves the different attitudes presented.

As readers progress through this volume, they are introduced to the various possibilities of aesthetic living represented by the characters: for example, the melancholy, romantic, reflective life of the narrator (presumably A himself) in "Diapsalmata"; the sensual pursuits of Don Juan in "The Immediate Stages of the Erotic"; and the "reflective grief" of the "Shadowgraphs." Each life highlights enjoyment—of a thought process, of language, of sexuality, of the moment, of the superficial. Notable for its absence, however, is life in the concrete; in a sense, all of the characters are shadowgraphs, for they represent abstract moods without concretion, or in Kierkegaardian terms, externality without true inwardness, mind without spirit. This moral judgment, of course, may not occur to the reader upon a first perusal.

Probably the most significant characterization in *Either* in terms of the reader's response is that of Johannes in "Diary of the Seducer." Representing the aesthetic existence carried to its logical extreme, Johannes is an artist who confuses his "art" with real life.[3] As he narrates his intricate plans for the seduction of Cordelia, for instance, he continually uses the terminology of art. Requiring continual "reflection" (1971, 1:431), he tells us overtly that he has made a "pact with the aesthetic" (1:432) in his relation to Cordelia. Expressing his disinterest in life, he asserts that he does not "care to possess a girl in the mere external sense, but enjoy her in the artistic sense" (1:368). Art is further emphasized when he examines his own method, questioning whether the "interesting" has "always been preserved" (1:432); in addition, he mentions the conventional artistic intent to unify: Cordelia's remarks are "the ends of the thread by which I weave her into my plan" (1:420); "when I have gazed and gazed again . . . then I shut up my fan, and gather the fragments into a unity, the parts into a whole" (1:423).

Like the creative writer, Johannes also uses figurative language:

similes and metaphors frequently describe his position ("serene I sit like the king of the cliff" [1971, 1:320]) or his method ("like an archer, I release the string, tighten it again, listen to its song, my battle ode, but I do not aim it yet, I do not even lay the arrow on the string" [1:345]). Interpreting Cordelia as if she were a "character" to him, he even calls attention to his own "heartless irony" (1:359). Indeed, his seemingly idealistic views of woman as an object of beauty, a "being for another" and the "dream of man" (1:425), are only more subtle forms of the ironic position: in effect, Johannes reduces the value of a real woman who could not measure up to this ideal. For the artistic seducer, as for the romanticist and the shadowgraph, the image replaces life in the concrete; art ("the glory and divinity of aesthetics" [1:423]) becomes their only god, and the result, Johannes indicates at the end of the diary after physical union has occurred, is a mood that Kierkegaard would interpret as despair.[4]

> Now all resistance is impossible, and only as long as that is present is it beautiful to love; when it is ended there is only weakness and habit. I do not wish to be reminded of my relation to her; she has lost the fragrance, and the time is past when a girl suffering the pain of a faithless love can be changed into a sunflower. (1:439)

But again the reader, even when viewing this final passage to the first volume, would not necessarily be aware that an ethical judgment is being implied.

Probably only in reading the second volume, the *Or* of this work, do the implications of the oppositional structure begin to unfold for the reader. Citing an example of the reader's progress toward awareness, Walter Lowrie relates in his biography of Kierkegaard that the reviewers of *Either/Or* were annoyed at first because "they were unable to understand what it was all about" ([1941] 1951, 149); "it was in the second part that Heiberg discovered a profundity of meaning which prompted him to counsel his readers to reread the first part and seek there a meaning which had likely escaped them, as it had escaped him" (p. 150).[5] *Or* contains the papers of B, in which another pseudonymous author, appropriately named Judge William, discusses the ethical and occasionally the religious way of life in two long letters written to A, the young aesthete of the first volume. The dialectical form begins to take shape early in the first letter when the judge says he intends to address A in a tone of "earnest admonition" (1971, 2:6). Shunning the indirect method of the historical author, B speaks directly to his friend in the grammatical second person and finds A guilty of living an "aesthetic" life of superficial drifting: "You abuse your gifts for irony and sarcasm by making mock of it"; "your life is wholly given over to preliminary runs"; "what you have a predilection for is the first sensation of falling in love"; "you love the accidental" (2:7). Later, B's counterposition is further enforced when he summarizes the moral problem he perceives with A's "aesthetic-intellectual intoxication":

> Every mood, every thought, good or bad, cheerful or sad, you pursue to its utmost limit, yet in such a way that this comes to pass rather *in abstracto* than *in concreto;* in such a way that this pursuit itself is little more than a mood from which nothing results but a knowledge of it. (2:17)

In contrast to A's presentation of woman as "the dream of man," the judge views her ethically as "the conscience of man" (2:68). Implicitly condemning the inconstancy of the seducer obsessed with his own artistry, B emphasizes marriage and "responsibility" as a "blessing and true joy" (2:87).

In B's second letter, the oppositional nature of the two existential possibilities becomes even more explicit as B continues his sermonizing, this time on the necessity of making a choice. But the decision, according to B, is not whether to choose good or evil; rather, it is "choosing to will" (2:173), for the aesthetic is "neutrality," a refusal to will, which implies a lack of consciousness of one's self "in one's eternal validity" (2:210). To achieve psychological and spiritual self-awareness, Judge William lectures repeatedly, is also to assume responsibility, to admit guilt, to repent; in brief, to choose oneself is to choose God (2:221). Yet such a choice, the judge warns, should not be an abstract one, such as a mystic undertakes.

> The mystic chooses himself abstractly. One can therefore say that he constantly chooses himself out of the world. But the consequence is that he is unable to choose himself back into the world. The truly concrete choice is that wherewith at the very same instant I choose myself out of the world I am choosing myself back into the world. For when I choose myself repentantly I gather myself together in all my finite concretion, and in the fact that I have chosen myself out of the finite I am in the most absolute contiguity with it. (2:253)

And so the judge implies that A makes no real choice, living instead in the abstract sphere of his art. But what would be the aesthete's rebuttal to the judge's lectures? Readers are never told. Confronted with two conflicting life possibilities, readers in the Kierkegaardian model of indirect communication are left to ponder their own choices. They receive little if any overt guidance in the text as to whether they should prefer the artistic but thoughtless and eventually heartless prowess of the aesthete or the seemingly deeper but often overbearing consciousness of a sometimes monotonous, occasionally insulting, but always judgmental moralist. Or perhaps they should choose both at different times or, as suggested later in *Stages on Life's Way*, neither of the two alternatives alone.

In *Stages on Life's Way* Kierkegaard posits as a third possibility the "religious" alternative, which dethrones (without totally eliminating) the aesthetic mode and which subsumes the ethical. In this existential mode, the individual achieves the eternal in the finite through faith. Kierkegaard's "religiousness A" in this category is the discovery of the eternal consciousness but with the mediation of a teacher (Christ); "religiousness B" is one's becoming conscious inwardly of the paradox between the eternal and the finite and accepting suffering because of the existential duty to the absolute.

This last plateau is approached imaginatively in *Stages on Life's Way* by the author of "Quidam's Diary," which purportedly was found in a box near a country lake by a Frater Taciturnus (1940, 183).[6] While the Chinese-box authorship as well as the diary form itself suggests an obvious parallel with "Diary of the Seducer" in *Either/Or* and while both narrators pass through the same external process of falling in love with a woman, courting her, and then leaving her, the two diaries nevertheless reveal vast differences in the internal attitudes of the narrators. The disinterested Johannes cares only about his own artistic prowess. Quidam, in contrast, manifests a deep awareness of God's presence in his life, accompanied by a genuine concern for the woman's welfare and an intense ambivalence about whether the religious individual should marry at all: "Dare a soldier on the frontier (spiritually understood) take a wife, a soldier . . . who, even though he does not fight day and night, though for a considerable period he has peace, yet never can know at what instant the war will begin again, since he cannot even dare to call this quiet a truce" (p. 188)? And most important, as one who approaches the religious sphere, Quidam also embraces suffering: "The loss of one's only wish is a thing one has to be prepared for if one would have to do with Him" (p. 224). Yet he suffers not so much by withdrawing from earthly concerns as by the torture of trying to deal with them in the concrete; that is, by attempting to realize an internal existence in the external world. This existential application, of course, is precisely what is missing in the aesthetic mode demonstrated by Johannes, while the element of suffering is notably absent from Judge William's personification of the ethical.

Hence, to return to *Either/Or*, the point is not simply to assume that true meaning lies in the position of the second of these volumes because it was written last (in fact, it was written first); rather, if Iser is correct, the point of an oppositional text is to develop the reader's own ability "to think in terms of alternatives . . . to visualize the possibilities [the characters] have not thought of [so that] the scope of [one's] judgment expands" (Iser 1978, 118). But most important, with this increase in power of judgment, the reader, Kierkegaard hopes, will not only be better able to reflect but will also, as Stephen Crites indicates (1972, 224), be moved by an existential crisis to act, to develop his or her own ethical/religious capability.

Thus, in the Kierkegaardian model of indirect communication, or more precisely, in any text using such a model, "a new species of moral drama" (Tompkins 1980, xv) rises from the ashes of the older, overtly didactic text of earlier centuries. In this newer mode, the real author is practically absent from the text, the implied author is relegated to a "structural principle" (Chatman 1978, 149), the narrators become mere embodiments of possibilities, and the reader is thereby challenged to achieve the utmost significance in the communication process. For the Christian artist this technique implies a belief in the ability of the individual to become a self, in his or her potential to achieve eternal validity. Thus, in spite of the pervading negativity that arises from Kierkegaard's widespread use of irony in *Either/Or*, the author's underlying positivity becomes visible through the reader-response mechanism. Kierkegaard's stance, in other words, shifts from negative to positive when the irony has "the positive function of stimulating a passionate search for meaning, purpose, and significance in regard to what is an 'object' of profound concern: one's own existence and the direction of one's life" (Stack 1977, 43). Moreover, the artist's intention here implies a basic sympathy with human nature generally and with the individual specifically—an attitude not present in a purely negative ironic model.

Precisely this model of indirect communication permeates Graham Greene's artistic intentions and shapes many of his novels. Like Kierkegaard, Greene seems to adopt an "artistic incognito," a habit of hiding behind what he calls the "facade of his public life" (1969, 41) and of refusing in direct communication such as autobiographies and interviews to accept the role of Christian authority.[7] A 1982 interview with Anthony Burgess, for example, includes one of his most recent statements concerning his Catholicism.

> I see we're getting on to myself as a Catholic novelist. I'm not that: I'm a novelist who happens to be a Catholic. The theme of human

beings lonely without God is a legitimate subject. To want to deal with the theme doesn't make me a theologian. Superficial readers say I'm fascinated by damnation. But nobody in my books is damned—not even Pinkie in *Brighton Rock*. Scobie in *The Heart of the Matter* tries to damn himself, but the possibility of his salvation is left open. The priest's final words are that nobody, not even the Church, knows enough about divine love and judgment to be sure that anyone's in hell. (Burgess 1982, 46–47)

A similar comment occurs in *Ways of Escape:*

My own course of life gave me no confidence in any aid I might proffer. I had no apostolic mission, and the cries for spiritual assistance maddened me because of my impotence. What was the Church for but to aid these sufferers? What was the priesthood for? I was like a man without medical knowledge in a village struck with plague. (Greene 1980b, 261)

Evident in both passages is a tone of humility, a leveling process that places the communicator on the same plateau with the recipient. The words echo Kierkegaard's denial, cited earlier, that he was an "apostle" or even a "teacher" and his claim of being only "a fellow student." This democratic pose is apparently essential to the indirect method: the author, as well as the characters, must be a human being like ourselves, capable of ignorance, weakness, failure; otherwise, readers will not need to question inadequate norms, recognize these norms as their own, and decide whether they can change these standards. The objection might be raised, however, that Greene's very abhorrence of the epithet "Catholic novelist" shows him opposed to any kind of communication with a moral aim—either directly or indirectly undertaken. But the objection will not stand, for what Greene dislikes about the label "Catholic novelist" lies in his assumption about what that title signifies, part of which is revealed in a reference he makes to Cardinal Newman.

Newman wrote the last word on "Catholic literature" in *The Idea of a University:* . . . "if Literature is to be made a study of human nature, you cannot have a Christian Literature. It is a contradiction in terms to attempt a sinless Literature of sinful man. You may gather together something very great and high, something higher than any Literature ever was; and when you have done so, you will find that it is not Literature at all." (1980b, 77-78)

Instead of being a writer of literature, Greene implies, the "Catholic novelist" to him is someone with authority, whose text incorporates norms which, though meritorious, may seem impossible to achieve, much less sustain; the text would then function as dogmatic and direct communication which could easily, as Kierkegaard so often pointed out, offend the recipient. Greene's novels, in contrast, seem to abdicate authority; they function not as moral or doctrinal teachings but much more indirectly as incitements to an awareness of moral capability or, in Kierkegaardian terms, as inducements to "subjectivity."

Yet, to state Greene's intention in this manner is not to deny his almost obsessive interest in moral and religious problems, and certainly it would be difficult to ignore the presence of those questions not only in many of his novels (*Brighton Rock, The Heart of the Matter, The Power and the Glory, The End of the Affair, A Burnt-Out Case, The Honorary Consul, Monsignor Quixote*, to cite only a few) but also in his essays, interviews, and autobiographies. But his interest might be more precisely described as a moral or "religious *sense*" (Greene 1969, 51; italics mine), an expression Greene himself has used in an essay on Henry James. Noting further that, for James, "religion was always a mirror of his experience" (p. 52), Greene explicitly questions the value of any organized philosophical or religious system in the novel; he cites Thomas Hardy as an example of the disadvantage of this type of proselytizing:

> If James had, like Hardy, tried to systematize his ideas, his novels too would have lurched with the same one-sided gait. They retain their beautiful symmetry at a price, the price which Turgenev paid and Dostoevsky refused to pay, the price of refraining from adding to the novelist's distinction that of a philosopher or a religious teacher of the second rank. (P. 53)

Like the moral and theological awareness of James and of Kierkegaard in his aesthetic works, then, Greene's ethical and religious sense arises from and applies to "existence," or, in the artist's terms, "experience"; he communicates it only indirectly, maintaining always the Kierkegaardian artistic disguise.

An intriguing sidelight to Greene's use of the concept of disguise appears as an epilogue to *Ways of Escape*. He entitles the anecdote "The Other" and begins by telling the reader that for many years he has been "in search of someone who called himself Graham Greene" (1980b, 311). Mentioning a poem by Edward Thomas called "The Other," Greene recalls portions of the verse in which the persona seems haunted by some other "I," an "other" whom he follows obsessively in an apparent effort to discover an identity with himself. A quarter of a century after reading the poem, Greene continues, he was shocked to discover that he, too, had an other, one who really existed—a thief, blackmailer, jailbreaker, and tramp—a deceiver who called himself Graham Greene and posed as a professional writer, causing a number of problems with government and civil authorities for the real Graham Greene. Over the years, the other made sporadic appearances in Greene's life, until a final confusion stunned him: "Some years ago in Chile, after I had been entertained at lunch by President Allende, a right-wing paper in Santiago announced to its readers that the President had been deceived by an impostor. I found myself shaken by a metaphysical doubt. Had *I* been the impostor all the time? Was I the Other?" (p. 320).

While any interpretation of this episode is, admittedly, sheer conjecture, the highlighting of the strange anecdote by placing it strategically as an epilogue to his autobiography certainly tempts one to wonder whether Greene is seriously troubled by the "deceptive" artistic pose he has maintained for so long. Has the disguise become the reality? Kierkegaard, it is interesting to note, was so concerned by his use of artistic disguise that, along with his use of indirect communication, he also wrote "edifying discourse" so that he would not be misunderstood; furthermore, in *Point of View* he stressed openly that he was, from the beginning, a religious author and that the aesthetic work was a deception for the truth's sake (1962a, 39–43). He did not, however, minimize the importance of his indirect method. But Greene, I think, is not likely to follow his predecessor's example of forthright explanation, for a reason that emphasizes an important difference between the two writers even within their similarity: by his own admission, Kierkegaard's religious aims were primary, his aesthetic interests ancillary, whereas Greene is primarily a novelist interested in the aesthetic; his goals, secondarily, seem to include the reader's moral and spiritual awakening. Both however, employ indirect communication in their attempts to reach these goals.

In Greene's fiction, signs of a movement toward a dialectical method may be discerned in *Brighton Rock*, an early novel containing discourse in which the implied author's voice, though still apparent, has already begun to fade into the background. Probably because the novel is narrated in the third person, though, some critics have assumed that the characters' distorted attitudes in this novel are views held also by the narrator and therefore by Greene.[8] If the assumption were valid, this novel and many others like it in the third person (*The Power and the Glory*, *The Honorary Consul*, for example), could not serve as examples of the indirect method, for Greene's direct voice would then interfere with the reader's independent progress toward self-formation.

A third-person narrator is not necessarily the "real" author, however, as numerous point-of-view studies have made clear (see, for example, Booth 1961 and Lanser 1981). But even more specific to the problem of confusion of attitudes in *Brighton Rock* is Roy Pascal's comprehensive analysis of "style indirect libre," or free indirect speech, in the novel. Pascal defines the technique:

> The narrator, though preserving the authorial mode throughout and evading the "dramatic" form of speech or dialogue, yet places himself, when reporting the words or thoughts of a character, directly into the experiential field of the character, and adopts the latter's perspective in regard to time and place. (1977, 9)

Practiced by such giants of the fictional world as Flaubert and James, the method would certainly be a familiar one to Greene, who has read the work of both novelists. In addition, the use of the technique apparently corresponds both with his attention to the reader's response in the communication process and with the general attitude of sympathy apparent in his work as a whole. Pascal believes that such an intention lies behind the use of the method: "Free indirect speech . . . necessarily implies a special concern for and intimacy with the character. The frequency of its incidence must affect the reader's response, since it tends to establish bonds not only of familiarity but also of sympathy" (p. 79).

The first part of the passage to which Turnell (1961) refers contains what Pascal defines as "simple" indirect speech, a form that is not really "free" (Pascal 1977, 8–9) because, though not direct dialogue, the speech is attached to a grammatical tag such as "said," "thought," or "remembered," as in "remembering the room at home, the frightening weekly exercise of his parents which he watched from his single bed" (Greene [1938] 1970, 108). But immediately following this sentence are two others without tags: "That was what they expected of you, every polony you met had her eye on the bed: his virginity straightened in him like sex. That was how they judged you: not by whether you had the guts to kill a man, to run a mob, to conquer Colleoni."

The implied author's voice, already beginning to fade in the first passage because the "frightening weekly exercise" is grammatically placed at some distance from the tag and in apposition with the intervening noun "room," becomes even less noticeable in the second passage, which has no tags. Since both the content and the diction ("polony," "guts") are clearly Pinkie's, not Greene's, the excerpt, with the exception of the simile, may be classified as an example of free indirect speech. Similar passages are repeated with some frequency throughout the novel: "If she were straight and loved him it would be just so much easier, that was all" ([1938] 1970, 255); "Kite had given him a cup of hot coffee and brought him here—God knows why—perhaps . . . because a man like Kite needed a little sentiment like a tart who keeps a pekinese" (p. 272). In these and other examples of free indirect speech, Greene allows the character a great deal of prominence so that he or she may reveal personal attitudes toward existence, subjective reasonings, rationalizations, and conclusions.

Of course, in this early novel the implied author's voice has by no means been eliminated. The interpretive omniscience of the narrator often intrudes in descriptive passages: "[Ida's] big breasts, which had never suckled a child of her own, felt a merciless compassion" ([1938] 1970, 148); "[Pinkie] had a deceptive sense of freedom as he walked softly down towards the Channel" (p. 234). Neither in *Brighton Rock* nor in other early novels such as *The Power and the Glory* or *The Heart of the Matter* are the lines of demarcation between the characters' existential perspectives so clearly drawn and so obviously dichotomous as they are in Kierkegaard's *Either/Or*. But the reader does become aware that several opposing attitudes toward life are present. Pinkie, for example, apparently believes in God but, despairing over his own salvation, lives the egoistic life of the aesthete which, in the exaggerated form that Pinkie espouses, leads to murder and suicide in a hopeless attempt to find internal peace. Greene's ironic posture toward the aesthete character is adopted not so much to denigrate the character as to offer the reader the opportunity to experience an attitude that leads to disaster in its exaggerated form. The thoughtful reader may then discover personally the horror of the aesthetic attitude which, as Judge William recognizes in *Either/Or*, leads to a figure like Nero who burned Rome "in order to get a conception of the conflagration of Troy" (Kierkegaard 1971, 2: 189).

Some alternatives to a totally egoistic form of the aesthetic existence in *Brighton Rock* include the lifestyle dramatized by Ida Arnold, the strictly conventional moralist who constantly prattles to Rose about Right and Wrong, becoming almost a parody of Kierkegaard's Judge William. With her inflexible clichés—"right's right, an eye for an eye" (Greene [1938] 1970, 276)—she judges Pinkie mercilessly but never internalizes her values as the true ethicist would. By insisting that she must rescue Rose from her husband's present and future violence, Ida denies the possibility of internal transformation: "Look at me, I've never changed. It's like those sticks of rock: bite it all the way down, you'll still read Brighton. That's human nature" (p. 247).

A third perspective is personified by Rose, who, though she never achieves true religiousness in Kierkegaard's sense, is conscious of her eternal being and is able to consider Pinkie's needs as well as her own. Certainly, too, she is an argument against the Freudian determinism that Pinkie seems to exemplify. Although she is a product of the same limited background that Pinkie is, she manages to achieve a sense of responsibility and maintains a hope for his transformation, while he continues in despair over his own guilt. Yet her willingness to risk her life and soul for him is an immolation rather than a Kierkegaardian realization of inner self.

After Pinkie's grotesque suicide, the novel ends ambiguously. Hope is expressed, on the one hand, by the possibility of a child and by the priest's comforting words to Rose, "You can't conceive, my child, nor can I or anyone—the . . . appalling . . . strangeness of the mercy of God" ([1938] 1970, 308), but despair threatens, on the other hand, as she walks home to listen to the record she has not yet heard, Pinkie's voice denying his love for her—"the worst horror of all" (p. 310).

Does Greene want the reader to believe in the possibility of human transformation? And which of these existential modes, if any, might he want the reader to choose? As in *Either/Or*, the object of choice is embedded not in the text but in the reader who reacts to the text, the reader who now may question his or her own beliefs about whether psychoethical change is possible. The resulting subjective confusion is what Greene hopes to incite by the indirect method. Marshall Brown states the process tellingly in an essay analyzing the dialectical imagination: "Feelings of disorientation and vertigo are a normal part of the processes of discovery; they constitute the inherently revolutionary element of dialectic, the dialectic element of revolution" (1984, 15). Like Kierkegaard, Greene thus tries to trick us out of our complacent way of thinking and into an existential crisis; through the act of reading, recipients in this communication process become free to imagine other existence possibilities—not only for the characters, but also for themselves. If *Brighton Rock* is read as the posing of a question, then, the ending may imply not a judgment of Pinkie, as many critics have assumed, but rather the impropriety of all judgment of one human being by another. As Greene himself replied in the interview cited earlier, "Nobody in my books is damned" (Burgess 1982, 47). Hence, beneath its external ironic stance, the novel reveals, early in Greene's career, a deep sympathy for the fallen person and a generally—albeit covertly—positive attitude expressed through his belief in the reader's ability to perform a liberating subjective act.

The dialectical method becomes most visible, however, in Greene's first-person narratives, in which he seems to have made a stronger effort to reduce overt signs of his own presence, so that, as author, he becomes "a mere medium through which truth manifests itself" (Kern 1970, 49). The narrator in these novels is usually an ironist, often an exaggerated artist-figure who reveals his ontological norms through his habits of discourse. In a more subtle version of the Conradian frame tale, Greene's first-person storyteller addresses not an overt listener but an implied reader. Of the several novels in Greene's canon illustrating this method, *The End of the Affair* is perhaps the clearest example and the one that most closely parallels Kierkegaard's use of a dichotomous dialectic in *Either/Or*.

Maurice Bendrix, as the first-person narrator and paradigm of the artist-figure, personifies Kierkegaard's aesthetic mode of living against the backdrop of a world war and its aftermath, when faith was a vanishing phenomenon. The opposing existential possibility arises through the character of Sarah Miles, whose progress to belief in spite of the world's disjunction contradicts Bendrix's exaggerated insistence on atheism.

Like Victor Eremita, who is intensely preoccupied with the symbolic secretary in *Either/Or*, Bendrix—not Greene, it is important to note—is obsessed with the art of writing. Calling attention to the story as story in the opening paragraph, he tells the reader immediately that he is a "professional writer who . . . has been praised for his technical ability"; he is aware of "images" ([1951] 1974, 1); he originally became acquainted with Sarah in order to use Henry, her civil-servant husband, as a model for a character in his newest novel (pp. 4–5). Recalling Johannes's "pact with the aesthetic," Bendrix reveals that writing is the foremost desire of his life: "For a few seconds I was happy—this was writing: I wasn't interested in anything else in the world" (p. 42).

As a writer, too, he echoes Kierkegaard's Johannes when he chooses techniques that preserve his ironic distance from his characters, even while emphasizing his artistic authority and thereby reminding the reader continually of his presence. One of the most blatant of these techniques is the use of the generalization, which "makes reference outward from the fictional to the real world . . . to 'universal truths'" (Chatman 1978, 22). Chatman points out further that this type of commentary, "since it is gratuitous, conveys the overt narrator's voice more distinctly than any feature short of explicit self-mention" (p. 228). In opposition to Greene's careful effacement of his own authorial presence, then, Bendrix imposes himself as artist upon the reader through assertions such as these: "Jealousy, or so I have always believed, exists only with desire" (Greene [1951] 1974, 40); "we are not hurt only by tragedy: the grotesque too carries weapons, undignified, ridiculous weapons" (p. 53); "disbelief could be a product of hysteria just as much as belief" (p. 156).

The simile, also used by Johannes, is a second artistic technique which appears quite frequently in Bendrix's discourse and serves again to underscore the narrator's intrusive artistry.[9] Some of these rhetorical figures seem intended mainly for a descriptive purpose: "I had fallen out of their sight as completely as a stone in a pond" ([1951] 1974, 4). Others, far more revealing of the narrator's own moral qualities, are reductive and judgmental toward the other characters: "Henry was important, but important rather as an elephant is important, from the size of his department" (p. 5); "at last

[Parkis] had really scented love and now he stalked it, his boy at his heels like a retriever" (p. 62); "she looked absurdly young, like a naked child" (p. 75); "[Father Crompton] had very limited small talk, and his answers fell like trees across the road" (p. 191). These similes seem intended to be creations of Bendrix rather than of Greene, who uses figurative language only rarely in his direct prose.

For Bendrix as artist, the simile appears to carry an additional function: "The simile always suggests that a pattern of relations in one context is similar to a pattern of relations in another and once such a connection has been made in thought, a step has been taken towards the building up of a wholeness more satisfying than the mere random togetherness of a collection of individual pars" (Dillistone 1955, 151). Bendrix thus uses the simile not only to judge and often to belittle the characters he talks about but also (though unconsciously) to bestow upon existence a unity that he feels it lacks. The process is another illustration of his artistic inclination to allow the abstract to emerge from the concrete: it is a passage away from existence and into thought—and a movement highly characteristic of the aesthete.

A third intrusive technique, and one that parallels Johannes's manipulation of Cordelia's emotions, is Bendrix's maneuvering of time in his narration. Susan Lanser's theory that "temporal distinctions are important indices of psychological and ideological relationships between the narrator and the story world" (1981, 199) is highly relevant here. In lieu of a purely linear narration, Bendrix begins his account with the statement that "a story has no beginning or end" (Greene [1951] 1974, 1); next, he describes his meeting with Henry in January 1946, a time already in the past. During the scene, he shifts still further back to 1939, the year when he first met Henry and Sarah. A few pages later, he returns to January and the scene with Henry, mentions a "future" that has also passed, and then begins again with several days or weeks (he can only guess) after the January night of his opening. Although the actual time of the writing, he informs us, is about three years after that night, the movement of narration back and then forward again to the same night both allows the time to seem more like a present action and highlights Bendrix's ability to control a story in much the same way as he controls the detective's investigations and, finally, even Sarah's cremation. He continues this temporal manipulation throughout the book, constantly reminding the reader, as Johannes does in *Either/Or*, not only of his presence but especially of his prowess.

But the temporal relation of narrator to narration may carry an even more important meaning if we apply Lanser's theory of ideological implication. By recalling his own past affair with Sarah, Bendrix seeks to render it eternally present through his act of writing. Thus, though he steadfastly fights, throughout the novel, against belief in an actual eternal God, Bendrix uses his art primarily to become godlike himself. His art then assumes the utmost significance, for it alone seems to sustain for him the elusive moment of his affair. Such a process highlights, however, not the affair but only the remembering of the affair; the narrator's attempt to control his life through art, therefore, is doomed to failure, for it produces an image when he desires a human being. In the typical aesthetic fashion that Judge William describes, the process allows the concrete matter of life to evaporate into an abstraction. Confronted with the failure of art to sustain the moment, both Johannes and Bendrix lapse into melancholy, the inevitable result, according to Kierkegaard, of functioning entirely on the aesthetic level. But while Johannes seems completely confined within that sphere, in the sense that he is unaware of alternate approaches to life, Greene's aesthetic man—perhaps because he is intended as a more rounded character to suit the needs of a novel—perceives, but struggles against, other possibilities outside his own.

The dialectical formation in the novel, accordingly, includes not only the opposition between Bendrix's mode of existence and Sarah's but also the tension between the narrator's past ironic attitude and his present realization of it. Bendrix thus maintains a double vision in the manner of Dickens's Pip or David Copperfield. On the one hand, Maurice depicts his own "record of hate" ([1951] 1974, 1) and "suspicion and envy" (p. 92); the reader watches him judge his characters patronizingly—"poor Sarah" (p. 63), "so stupidly loyal" (p. 66), Parkis, "so timid" (p. 39)—and he embarrasses Parkis (p. 39) and hurts Henry by telling him that Sarah had slept with many other lovers (p. 198). Some of his worst insults, almost comically, are addressed to the God he insists he does not believe in. On the other hand, by becoming aware of his own ironic stance, he is able to move to the edge of the aesthetic sphere where, realizing his emptiness, he occasionally tries to fill the void by showing sympathy for other characters (p. 143) or by stifling a brutal revelation (p. 145) that would have caused more pain.

In spite of his negative stance, too, the positive values he has evidently submerged are revealed through the qualities he notices and praises in the other characters and sometimes even in himself: "Why should I say poor Henry? Didn't he possess in the end the winning cards—the cards of gentleness, humility and trust?" ([1951] 1974, 24); "it occurred to me with amazement that for ten minutes I had not thought of Sarah or of my jealousy; I had become nearly human enough to think of another person's trouble" (p. 40). By the time of Sarah's funeral, moreover, he has progressed to the crucial point of realizing the difference between life and art: "It pleased me . . . [that] I was a human being to her and not a writer: a man whose friends died and who attended their funerals, who felt pleasure and pain, who might even need comfort, not just a skilled craftsman" (p. 162). At the same time, he comes to the melancholy awareness of himself as an aesthete—though he does not use the term—whose work had become an obsession to divert his mind:

> I recognized my work for what it was—as unimportant a drug as cigarettes to get one through the weeks and years. . . . If we are extinguished by death, as I still try to believe, what point is there in leaving some books behind any more than bottles, clothes or cheap jewelry? And if Sarah is right, how unimportant the importance of art is. (P. 161)

He may even suspect his own moral capability, in fact, which becomes evident in a metaphorical passage when he pauses from his aesthetic pursuit to regard himself for a moment subjectively:

When I began to write I said this was a story of hatred, but I am not convinced. Perhaps my hatred is really as deficient as my love. I looked up just now from writing and caught sight of my own face in a mirror close to my desk, and I thought, does hatred really look like that? For I was reminded of that face we have all of us seen in childhood, looking back at us from the show-window, the features blurred with our breath, as we stare with such longing at the bright unobtainable objects within. ([1951] 1974, 58)

Apparently because he assumes that the ethical/religious potential buried within him is unrealizable, though, Bendrix stops short of choosing the leap into theological belief (p. 209) that, according to Kierkegaard, could rescue him from a purely aesthetic existence.

Sarah Miles disputes her lover's assumption in her oppositional role as the newly converted ethical/religious individual in the novel. Greene again uses first-person narration as an indirect method dramatizing her viewpoint, this time in the form of her diary which Parkis has stolen for Bendrix to read. Like Bendrix, Sarah begins in the aesthetic stage as a victim of her own sensuality. Married to the dull Henry Miles, she finds diversion and even excitement in a sexual relationship with Maurice; like him, she uses writing to recreate the affair—"As long as I go on writing, yesterday is today and we are still together" ([1951] 1974, 96). As with Bendrix's narration, the first-person diary form vocalizes the tension of her shifting stance. Vacillating continually between irony and acceptance, doubt and belief, hatred and love, struggle and internal peace, she seems a paradigm of the Kierkegaardian mobile standpoint. But though aware of the fragmentation and emptiness in the world and herself, as underscored by the frequency of desert imagery in the diary (pp. 94, 97, 104, for example), she nevertheless responds to the crisis of finding the "dead" Bendrix alive by choosing God—whom she finds within her own consciousness by exerting her will to believe.

Her choice crystallizes the oppositional perspective in the text, for the decision propels her into the Kierkegaardian ethical/religious existence, where she experiences the suffering characteristic of that sphere: "Now the agony of being without him [Bendrix] starts" ([1951] 1974, 100). But here the vacillation continues, though it arises from a different cause, for to Kierkegaard and to Greene, positing a belief is not at all identical with living a belief. Sarah's diary entry of February 1946, recorded a year and a half after she had first chosen belief, indicates that struggle "against the loss of one's only wish" (Kierkegaard 1940, 224) persists in spite of her resolution: "I'm tired and I don't want any more pain. I want Maurice. I want ordinary corrupt human love. Dear God, you know I want to want Your pain, but I don't want it now. Take it away for a while and give it me another time" (Greene [1951] 1974, 131).

The subject of this passage also implies an important difference between Bendrix's narration and Sarah's, for while his obsession with the abstract enjoyment of art tends to resemble that of Johannes in "Diary of the Seducer," her attention later in the diary to the immense chasm between abstract virtue and its appropriation in existence seems closer to the concern of "Quidam" in Kierkegaard's *Stages on Life's Way*. Like "Quidam," after withdrawing from the object of her sensual pursuit, she displays a sincere concern for Bendrix's welfare; along with her counterpart, she demonstrates an apparently unmediated awareness of the paradox between the eternal and the finite inherent in Kierkegaard's "religiousness B." And like "Quidam"—though unlike Bendrix—she accepts suffering as the inevitable result of her choice. Bendrix does not escape suffering, of course. Indeed, as the priest recognizes during his final visit with Henry and Maurice, Bendrix is a man suffering the intense pain that arises from his own ironic position. Without comment, Greene allows the character's perspective to disclose its own disastrous effects.

The author's spatial arrangement of these opposing perspectives in the text, though, differs strikingly from Kierkegaard's. *Either/Or*, taken as a whole, contains a lateral placement of the two opposing views. In *The End of the Affair*, the diary (or the religious mode) is placed significantly in the physical center of Maurice's narration (or the aesthetic sphere). In a highly appropriate sexual metaphor—and here Greene's subtlety and indirection triumph—the narrator's own text takes on a feminine shape: Sarah, through her diary, penetrates Maurice's ironic/aesthetic attitude with her religious acceptance of a hated self, so that she assumes the active (if stereotypically masculine) role of choosing, while Bendrix unwittingly remains the passive recipient who dares not leap, who fears to choose himself and God. Yet he does awaken, if only to the consciousness that, by hating or by his ironic attitude, he hovers on the brink of belief. The metaphor, I think, is an analogue of how Kierkegaard in *Either/Or* and Greene in *The End of the Affair* covertly use the maieutic method to affect their recipients: as the text penetrates the mind of the complacent individual, he or she will awaken to consider the question of choice and, after experiencing the negativity of the purely ironic attitude, progress toward a decision that Kierkegaard and Greene believe to be the only possible means of establishing real control (as opposed to artistic control) over one's life. The dialectical method, when used with this intention, reflects again the belief of the Christian artist—this time in the human potential to achieve ethical/religious "capability."

I do not imply that the novel is a diatribe against art; Greene as well as Kierkegaard is certainly controlling our responses, and both clearly are prolific artists who seem to enjoy writing for its own sake in addition to employing it as a vehicle for moral or religious goals. But what the novel suggests about the opposition between art and religion is perhaps best stated by Johannes Climacus, Kierkegaard's pseudonym in *Concluding Unscientific Postscript:* "The maximum of attainment is simultaneously to sustain an absolute relationship to the absolute end, and a relative relationship to relative ends" (1968c, 371). The dialectic in this novel, therefore, is not art versus Christianity but the obsessive use of art as a substitute for life versus the appropriation of thought into existence. Maurice's narration, like Johannes's in *Either/Or*, leads to passivity, lack of choice, melancholy, and emptiness; Sarah's writing acts as a vehicle through which she achieves self-recognition and genuine, existential control. Later in Greene's career, he places the opposing perspectives into the mouths of more minor characters, such as Jones in *The Comedians* or even Wordsworth in *Travels with My Aunt*, but in *The End of the Affair*, the major characters speak forcefully in a text dichotomously arranged to highlight the crisis of choice. In this form of indirect communication, the reader must then decide, as Greene would have it, either to choose belief or else to continue in despair.

3

The Force of Ambiguity: Politics and the Individual

In her essay on the sociopolitical involvement of writers of fiction, Margaret Laurence points out that "no novelist writes in an objective way, if indeed there is anywhere such a mode of writing. The novelist takes a stand, and this is what makes us so vulnerable" (1978, 16). The stand, of course, may appear in any number of different guises: a rather direct voice—an opinionated third-person narrator who does not participate in the story, for example—or perhaps a character who is obviously intended as a norm. But often, especially in relatively modern political fiction, the commentary is more indirect, adopting the guise of a sustained ironic presentation of a governmental or social situation made to appear stupid *(Gulliver's Travels, The Ordeal of Richard Feverel)*, threatening *(Nineteen Eighty-Four, Brave New World)*, or starkly tragic *(The Red Badge of Courage, A Farewell to Arms)*. Clearly, the reader experiences in these novels a confrontation with the dramatized results of political or social problems, rather than a theoretical description of the problems themselves; moreover, the implied author is often condemning, in addition to the particular local, national, or international examples of partisan politics, the perennial or universal acts of human brutality—war, persecution, civil antagonism, official manipulation, or almost any form of social injustice. Astute readers who can interpret such devices as allegory, imagery, and characterization and who can use their own norms to judge these acts will generally experience little difficulty in pinpointing this type of implicit "political" opinion, even without hearing the author's more direct, nonironic voice.

According to this rather broad interpretation of authorial politics, most of Graham Greene's novels—and perhaps much of modern fiction as well—can probably be categorized as "political." More useful for literary criticism, however, is a somewhat narrower definition, though not one that is restricted to specific types of governmental affairs. I will use "political" to refer to novels concerned with state or church government, with social or public issues, or with the affairs of any establishment. Certainly, I do not mean to suggest that Greene's political novels are disguised propaganda; as Laurence further insists, a novelist "usually does not and should not write in any polemical way. . . . We do not presume to tell the reader how to think, nor can we offer any easy solutions" (1978, 16). While Greene's fiction shows concern for particular social problems, he nevertheless maintains the indirect method of communication in these books. But whereas in several of the religious novels he chooses the Kierkegaardian dialectical structure as his form, in the political fiction, he seems to prefer another type of indirection which Kierkegaard also employs: the deliberate creation of ambiguity (Anderson 1966, 243) through a kind of thematic double cross. In *Training in Christianity*, Kierkegaard specifies the process, always emphasizing its intent to efface the presence of the communicator:

> Indirect communication can be produced by the art of reduplicating the communication. This art consists in reducing oneself, the communicator, to nobody, something purely objective, and then incessantly composing qualitative opposites into unity. This is what the pseudonyms are accustomed to call "double reflection." An example of such indirect communication is, so to compose jest and earnest that the composition is a dialectical knot—and with this to be nobody. If anyone is to profit by this sort of communication, he must undo the knot for himself. Another example is, to bring defence and attack

together in such a unity that no one can say directly whether one is attacking or defending, so that both the most zealous partisans of the cause and its bitterest enemies can regard one as an ally—and with this to be an objective something, not a personal man. (1944b, 132–33)

The *Concluding Unscientific Postscript* offers an example of both the jest/earnest and the attack/defense models of communication. Calling himself a humorist, Johannes Climacus nevertheless spends hundreds of pages apparently in earnest, painstakingly building up his rational argument in defense of subjective Christianity, expounding on views that match those of Kierkegaard in the direct prose of the *Journals;* yet, in the appendix, Climacus apparently attacks his own icon by revoking everything he has just written:

> So then the book is superfluous; let no one therefore take the pains to appeal to it as an authority; for he who thus appeals to it has *eo ipso* misunderstood it. To be an authority is far too burdensome an existence for a humorist . . . so what I write contains also a piece of information to the effect that everything is so to be understood that it is understood to be revoked, and the book has not only a Conclusion but a Revocation. (1968c, 546–47)

The method confuses: the reader may wonder at the end whether the apparently earnest treatise is a mere linguistic trick, whether the book is a defense of or an attack on subjective Christianity. But the *Journals* (4:4534–84; 2:2110–36) indicate that the real object of Kierkegaard's attack is not the subjective Christian but the person (Johannes Climacus) who merely philosophizes about subjective Christianity. Kierkegaard defends a personal existence that becomes Christian in its essential as well as its accidental properties through the development of "inwardness": "The supplicant does not seek god in the external world, does not create him in his desires, but finds him in his inwardness" (1967–78, 2:2114). One cannot become an ethical or religious individual through a direct external communication or, more specifically, by following someone else's abstract theory or by reading Johannes's book. What matters instead, according to

Kierkegaard, is one's application of Christian principles to *oneself* in concrete, everyday existence.

The *Attack upon "Christendom,"* a collection of short diatribes, illustrates further this interlocking technique. Viewing established church officials as self-deceived functionaries who lull their parishioners into a sense of false security, Kierkegaard published scathing articles first in the *Fatherland,* a prominent political journal, and later in the *Instant,* deploring the comfortable life of church officials and lashing out at what he called the illusion that what is preached in Danish churches is Christianity or that all who were baptized there could be considered Christians. The specific event that set off the series of outbursts was Professor Hans Martensen's praise of Bishop Mynster, former preacher and minister of Kierkegaard's church.[1] The eulogy, delivered just after the bishop's death, called him a "witness to the truth." Kierkegaard objected angrily to the label, pointing out that Mynster's life of enjoyment signaled an abstract rather than a concrete Christianity; his sermons, too, lacked existential reality because they regularly omitted "that part of Christianity which has to do with dying from the world" ([1944a] 1968, 5). The harsh criticism in this article and in the essays that followed led many of Kierkegaard's contemporaries to assume that, after spending a lifetime attending church services, he had now turned decisively against the Church of Denmark. The final proof, they assumed, lay in his radical exhortation to the people:

> Whoever thou art, whatever in other respects thy life may be, my friend, by ceasing to take part (if ordinarily thou dost) in the public worship of God, as it now is (with the claim that it is the Christianity of the New Testament), thou hast constantly one guilt the less, and that a great one: thou dost not take part in the treating God as a fool by calling that the Christianity of the New Testament which is not the Christianity of the New Testament. (P. 59)

In the translator's introduction to *Attack upon "Christendom,"* Lowrie demonstrates how the real meaning of the book became distorted: though it was Kierkegaard's last work, it was the first to be translated and published in Germany and in most other countries except for England and the United States ([1944a] 1968, xi). Removed thus from the context of his earlier thought, Lowrie says, the work was grasped by those with "an anticlerical if not an anti-Christian interest" and was, not surprisingly, "misapprehended in lands where [Kierkegaard's] works were unknown and little or nothing was known about the man" (p. xi).[2] That is, while Kierkegaard was attacking the unexamined living of the Danish Lutheran clergy and the complacent lay members of an established church consumed by external theories of Christian life, he was at the same time vigorously defending what he called "the true Christianity" (p. 55), an existence clearly marked, according to Kierkegaard, by suffering rather than by enjoyment and by a deep, subjective awareness of one's relationship to the Absolute, or the eternal Being.

The misapprehension of the meaning of *Attack upon "Christendom,"* in fact, serves only to confirm Kierkegaard's assertion about the potential outcome of an indirect political technique: from the results of the communication, the communicator can succeed "in ascertaining which is which, who is the believer, who the freethinker; for this is revealed by the way they judge the production which is neither attack nor defense" (1944b, 133). His method is thus not solely to attack or merely to defend: it is both, but not in any narrowly partisan sense. Kierkegaard, as is evident in article after article in *Attack upon "Christendom,"* is not interested in the details of who should publicly run the Danish church or the question of how many baptized persons can qualify as participants in it or even the specific topic of each sermon. Instead, as the above quotation seems to imply, he is concerned with the individual's subjective existence and therefore with each reader's reaction to his production. His national and church "politics," then, amount to his hope for the reader's personal development of a less aesthetic, more ethical/religious existence within the church, an intention that his earlier work clearly substantiates. His political position, moreover, is similar to his standpoint of mobile irony: the emptiness and hypocrisy of the contemporary established church represent his larger worldview of disjunction; his defense of what he calls "true" Christianity indicates his positive belief in human transformation undertaken from within and then manifesting itself externally. The topical situation attains significance, therefore, only in relation to the individual's reaction to it.

One final illustration of the attack/defense method occurs in *Training in Christianity*. In a comment which appeared later, Kierkegaard explains his technique in this work.

> If the Establishment can be defended at all, this is the only way, namely, by pronouncing a judgment upon it poetically (therefore by a pseudonym), thus drawing upon "grace" raised to the second power, in the sense that Christianity would not be forgiveness merely for what is past, but by grace would be a sort of dispensation from following Christ in the proper sense and from the effort properly connected with being a Christian. In that way truth would enter the Establishment after all: it defends itself by condemning itself; it acknowledges the Christian requirement, makes for its own part an admission of its distance from the requirement that it is not even an effort in the direction of coming closer to it, but has recourse to grace "also with respect to the use one makes of grace." ([1944a] 1968, 54)

Essentially, *Training in Christianity* consists of an explanation of how and why the individual's relation with Christ may come into conflict with the established church. Objecting to what he saw as the tendency in his age to consider a sociopolitical establishment as central (see Malantschuk's Commentary in Kierkegaard 1967–78, vol. 4, p. 665), Kierkegaard—without denigrating the necessity or the importance of an established social unit—emphasized again the primary importance of the individual: "The Inviter must invite all, yet every one severally as an individual . . . [even] the most solitary of all fugitives!" (1944b, 16).[3] And this emphasis on the personal in the text also functions as a kind of metaphor of Kierkegaard's authorial relationship to the single reader, in particular in this case to

Bishop Mynster, whose reaction he would consider typical of the rest of the established church:

> I ventured to give the matter [i.e., *Training in Christianity*] this turn, in order to see what the old Bishop would do about it. If there was power in him, he must do one of two things: *either* declare himself decisively for the book, venture to go with it, let it count as the defense which would ward off the accusation against the whole official Christianity which the book implies poetically, affirming that it is an optical illusion, "not worth a sour herring"; *or* attack it as decisively as possible, brand it as a blasphemous and profane attempt, and declare that the official Christianity is the true Christianity. He did neither of the two, he did nothing; and it became clear to me that he was impotent. ([1944a] 1968, 55)

The passage identifies three possible responses to the attack/defense method: readers may attack the pseudoauthor's text, defend it, or become paralyzed by it. In the first two instances, they would be reduplicating the real author's own method and, at the very least, would be forced to examine their own positions. In the last of the three responses, readers would be revealing the refusal to make any kind of moral commitment which is characteristic of the Kierkegaardian aesthete and which implies a lack of the individuality that the author tries to foster not only in *Training in Christianity* but also in much of his other writing (1967–78, 2:1964–2086, for example).

Despite all the attention he lavishes upon the individual's relationship with God, however, and regardless of his railings against the Church of Denmark, in one sense Kierkegaard also defends organized religion. He tries to cleanse the church by tearing away the hypocrisy that he feels is the infectious disease of the liturgical organization; he attempts a purification by dethroning the Hegelian deification of an established order (1944b, 88) grown undeserving, "the invention of the indolent worldly mind, which would put itself at rest and imagine that all is sheer security and peace, that now we have reached the highest attainment" (p. 89). Even as he attacks the complacency of a contemporary church that seems to consider itself "triumphant," he assumes the possibility of a different kind of establishment by recalling "the age when the church was militant" (p. 211) or when it existed in "fear and trembling" (p. 89), as some individuals did and, he believed, still can do. Politically, then, Kierkegaard's intention actually seems not only positive but particularly enterprising: he wants to raise the status of the individual within the organization, to emphasize the truth that the formation of a personal relationship with God, which includes constant suffering and striving, is not simply an attitude or a pose but a real ethical/religious action that can form the basis of a worthy social establishment. In short, the texts of *Concluding Unscientific Postscript* and, more emphatically, those of *Attack upon "Christendom"* and *Training in Christianity* simultaneously attack and defend; though seemingly focused negatively on topical issues, their thrust also reflects a positive belief in a reader's ability to effect personal change. Such change, though, requires that each reader shed complacency, perhaps undergo confusion and anxiety, and respond to the text as an individual whose life is somehow deeply involved with the issues at stake.

In several of Greene's political novels, he too seems to use the attack/defense model to "irritate" or "stimulate" (Anderson 1966, 284) readers into exploring their own degree of commitment. And as with Kierkegaard's use of the method, a sufficient amount of ambiguity results in the fiction, which forces readers to decide whether an attack or a defense has been mounted on the object. *The Quiet American*, a Vietnam war novel, is one of the clearest examples of this mode, sparking probably the widest range of conflicting critical opinions of all Greene's novels, and continually raising the subject of who or what is being attacked and/or defended. Various critiques of the novel have appealed to virtually the same evidence to support diametrically opposite conclusions. Predictably, too, many critics end by taking sides themselves, revealing their own emotional or political commitment or even stating a personal belief. Earlier critics, writing within a few years of the book's publication in 1955, tended to read it as an attack on American policy in Vietnam and a defense of British neutrality. Robert Evans, for example, finds that Greene characterizes the American, Alden Pyle, as "insidious" and "naive," while picturing the Britisher, Thomas Fowler, though not sinless, still "courageous because he has the intelligence to realize what he is making of himself" (1957, 243). Insisting further that Fowler's "desire to get Phuong back bears no causal relationship with the death of Pyle," Evans attempts to win even more sympathy for Greene's narrator by also pointing out that "throughout the novel he suffers" and therefore is "not incapable of feeling pain" (p. 244). Although the critic states that we should not necessarily assume Greene's anti-Americanism from these portraits that bear national overtones, Evans nevertheless concludes that the author "must have felt . . . we deserved criticism" (p. 247).

Nathan A. Scott interprets Pyle similarly as displaying an "insensibility" and an "ignorance of concrete political realities," even blaming the American for causing Fowler (whose character the critic does not analyze) to "betray his neutralism" (1956, 901). But Scott carries what he sees as Greene's attack on America much further from the novel than does Evans. Since "at no point in the book are any of the other characters allowed really to challenge Fowler," Scott accuses Greene of "splattering . . . gross nonsense across the entire book and making it clear that he prefers the absurd picture of American civilization that just now so many European intellectuals cling to" (p. 902). Maintaining that Greene's picture of American life is "absurd" is, of course, the result of the critic's measuring his own defensive image of the United States against that of Fowler's. As a reader, this critic has probably revealed more of his own commitment or belief than has Greene as author.

Writing a full twenty years later, at a time when the opinion of many Americans had shifted to oppose our involvement in Vietnam, Eric Larsen also views Greene as attacking Pyle and, by extension, America; this critic concludes, however, that the author's "analysis of the American motivation in that war is not really, in the end, trite or shallow or irresponsible but rather unpleasantly accurate" (1976, 41). All three of these critics clearly view the novel as an attack on the American presence in Vietnam, but the response to Greene's alleged attack varies between acceptance and outrage, depending more heavily upon the critic's own convictions than on the text itself, which has obviously stimulated readers to analyze their own positions.

One's awareness of the ambiguity in this novel increases when opposing critical responses are noted. An essay by Trilling and Rahv (1956) is revealing; Diana Trilling's conventional reading of Greene's anti-Americanism and even pro-Communism in the book is militantly countered by Philip Rahv's response, which, while not denying the presence of anti-Americanism in the book, indicates that it is the narrator, Thomas Fowler, "who is the mouthpiece of the anti-American sentiments which Mrs. Trilling finds so offensive." What is worse, Rahv insists, Mrs. Trilling "appraises this anti-Americanism as Communist in essence" (1956, 69). Rahv is one of a minority of earlier critics who perceived both personal and political motives beneath Fowler's complicity in Pyle's murder; he sees Fowler, rather than Greene, as the neutralist. Anthony Burgess concurs that "the anti-Americanism of the book springs from the natural jealousy and vindictiveness of the narrator" (1967, 96). One of the fictitious disputants in Laurence Lerner's rather curious dialogic article likewise maintains, in opposition to another participant in the debate, that since "Greene has gone out of his way to throw doubt on Fowler's motives for having Pyle killed," we should "equally throw doubt on his [Fowler's] political wisdom" (1964, 136).

While critics rarely agree on *all* particulars, the conflicting commentaries seem to demonstrate, at the very least, the difficulty of grasping even a basic meaning from the text itself. If we assume that the ambiguity is purposeful, then Greene's attack/defense method is a deliberate attempt to throw responsibility onto the individual reader/critic, who in turn, as in the Kierkegaardian mode, is offered the opportunity of "becoming," a process not unlike the kind of undertaking that Stanley Fish describes when he urges a critical examination that is centered less on the text and more on the reader.

> In the procedures I would urge, the reader's activities are at the center of attention, where they are regarded, not as leading to meaning, but as *having* meaning. The meaning they have is a consequence of their not being empty; for they include the making and revising of assumptions, the rendering and regretting of judgments, the coming to and abandoning of conclusions, the giving and withdrawing of approval, the specifying of causes, the asking of questions, the supplying of answers, the solving of puzzles . . . these activities . . . are at every moment settling and resettling questions of value. (1980, 172)

This constant flurry of reader activity in the model Fish presents is essentially a continual "re-vision," the espousing of always differing views; the process, he assumes, can occur to some degree as a response to any text. But I suggest that, for the political writings of Kierkegaard and Greene, the revision process may be greatly intensified in the reader because attack and defense are so intricately blended by the writer. Such interweaving produces, inevitably, a variety of critical responses, either in the individual reader or, in the case of Greene's novel, also in a number of different readers who react to the same evidence. Such responses help to explain the controversies that surround the political works of both authors.

Greene sometimes combines the attack and defense not only within the same text but even within the same character. In *The Quiet American*, the ambiguity of Pyle's characterization is an outstanding example of the double-edged method. Viewing him from the position of a reader, I find, like the narrator (and of course, partially because of the narrator), that the American's positive features are difficult to deny. Introducing him, Fowler describes Pyle as "quiet," "modest," "very, very serious"; he "criticised nobody" and was so scrupulously honest that no sooner had he claimed to know the writer York Harding than he immediately corrected the false impression saying, "I don't know him well . . . I guess I only met him twice"; the narrator helps form the reader's view at this point by saying, "I liked him for that" ([1955] 1973, 16). Pyle's veracity becomes more strikingly apparent when he risks death by pursuing Fowler into Vietminh territory in order to confess that he had "fallen in love with Phuong" (p. 58), Fowler's Vietnamese girlfriend and sexual partner. Furthermore, the young American demonstrates courage and leadership when he pounces on the tower guard, "pulling the sten to his side of the room" (p. 106). And again at great risk to himself, he actually saves Fowler's life by returning to find and carry him to safer ground when the Britisher lay injured and vulnerable within the range of the Viets' bombings.

Throughout the story, the narrator is attracted, as many readers may be, to the American's youth and freshness, the marital stability he offers Phuong, his sincerity, his concern for other people, his steadfast friendship with Fowler in spite of the latter's anger and cynicism, and, above all, his apparently blameless motivation, even in the face of its sometimes fatal results. "Oh, I know your motives are good," Fowler grudgingly admits, though not without some irony; "they always are" ([1955] 1973, 148).

Yet, if Greene defends Pyle for his traditional Christian virtues, he simultaneously attacks him (and, by extension, America) for what may be an avoidable ignorance that leads to emotional and physical injury, destruction, and death. Involved in the implementation of General Thé's "Third Force" tactics, Pyle tries to apply to the Vietnamese debacle the abstract principles he has read about in York Harding's books. The actual results are stunning. Fowler describes the aftermath of the bombings that took place in a popular area where hundreds of civilians habitually shop and dine: "Bits of cars were scattered over the square, and a man without his legs lay twitching at the edge of the ornamental gardens. . . . A woman sat on the ground with what was left of her baby in her lap . . . what struck me most in the square was the silence" ([1955] 1973, 180, 182). In the portrayal of senseless civilian casualties, the huge discrepancy that Kierkegaard emphasized in *Concluding Unscientific*

Postscript between the existential reality of life and the abstractness of thought and writing is dramatized grotesquely; a reader who has admired Pyle may now be forced into taking a different view of him.

But the process does not end here, for the narrator continues to praise and blame the American throughout the entire story. In one representative passage, Fowler reveals the vacillation which, in this instance, leans in Pyle's favor:

> All the time that his innocence had angered me, some judge within myself had summed up in his favour, had compared his idealism, his half-baked ideas founded on the works of York Harding, with my cynicism. Oh, I was right about the facts, but wasn't he right too to be young and mistaken, and wasn't he perhaps a better man for a girl to spend her life with? ([1955] 1973, 175)

But the scales shift and reshift yet again when the supposedly neutral Britisher subsequently arranges with a Chinese communist underground group to have Pyle murdered in order to stop people from dying "for his mistakes" (p. 193)—and then experiences guilt for having judged him.

The ambiguity is further heightened through a repetition of the attack/defense method in the characterization of Fowler himself. On the one hand, and again possibly because of the first-person narration, many readers tend to sympathize with Fowler, as much of the earlier critical response has demonstrated. Certainly, he appreciates the chasm between what he terms a "mental concept" ([1955] 1973, 98) and the incorporation of that concept into an individual's existence. An experienced reporter, Fowler has lived in Vietnam far longer than has Pyle and has been able to observe the destruction firsthand. He embodies Christian values when he deplores the practice of war; he is pained by the youth of the guards in the tower and feels sadness for being even indirectly responsible for their deaths; he shows sympathy for the many Vietnamese people who, he says, simply "want enough rice. . . . They don't want to be shot at. They want one day to be much the same as another. They don't want our white skins around telling them what they want" (pp. 99–100).

On the other hand, Fowler's weaknesses are also indicated in the text, often by himself as the narrator. Though he values Pyle's truthfulness, for instance, Fowler habitually lies. He tries (unsuccessfully) to convince Vigot, the police detective, that Pyle did not visit the Rue Catinat on the night of the murder; he deceives both Phuong and Pyle about the transfer to England and deliberately fails to tell them that his wife refuses to grant him a divorce. Even more damaging by Fowler's own standard, though, is his tendency to deceive himself, a weakness he recognizes only after Pyle has been killed. The most obvious example of his self-deception is the often-repeated assertion of his objectivity: "I was a reporter, I had no real opinions about anything" ([1955] 1973, 72); "politics . . . don't interest me . . . I'm not *engagé*" (p. 102); "I'm not involved" (p. 169). But in spite of his protestations, many readers have discerned that he *is* involved. Pyle's murder not only is a sociopolitical act of complicity with communistic interests but may also be a personally expedient move—Pyle's death reopens the possibility of Phuong's return and, with it, the opportunity for sexual satisfaction and social security to ward off the threatening specters of old age and loneliness.

Fowler's weaknesses extend to other areas, too, widening the basis for Greene's attack against his moral credibility. Significantly, the narrator's most serious objection to Pyle—his failure to understand the (Kierkegaardian) difference between the abstract and the concrete—becomes in the text a standard that, ironically, the reader may also use to measure Fowler himself. By this norm, one can discern the charges against Pyle being subtly reduplicated in the characterization of Fowler. Blinded by his own theoretical assumptions, he fails like Pyle to notice pain in its concrete forms. Before receiving his wife's emotional letter, for instance, the cynical Britisher had not considered that she would suffer from the manner in which he requested a divorce. And only much later does he discover that his stereotypical assumptions about the simplicity and toughness of Vietnamese women had caused him to miss the vulnerability hidden by Phuong's inability to articulate her emotional needs: "One never knows another human being; for all I could tell, she was as scared as the rest of us: she didn't have the gift of expression, that was all" ([1955] 1973, 149).

The exchange with Granger near the end of the novel most clearly highlights the similarity of Pyle and Fowler, when the latter's denigration of everything American prompts him to perceive Granger as an "emblematic statue" ([1955] 1973, 206) in an "alcoholic fog" (p. 204). Stunned by Granger's revelation that he is not drunk but is terribly frightened because his son is in danger of dying from polio, Fowler at last realizes the extent of his own blindness and sadly recalls the scene in which Pyle had been startled to discover the blood on his shoe after the bombing. "Was I so different from Pyle, I wondered? Must I too have my foot thrust in the mess of life before I saw the pain?" (p. 208).

In still another parallel with the characterization of Pyle, Fowler too permits the death of the innocent, while he remains, like the clergy in Kierkegaard's *Attack upon "Christendom,"* comfortable in his neutralist principles. He rides along and articulates no protest against the napalm bombing raid that must have killed a number of civilians. And like the American, Fowler also causes suffering, for he precipitates Pyle's death. The only difference between Fowler's own act and Pyle's involvement in the "bicycle" bombs, the former realizes at length, is quantitative: Pyle damaged the lives and families of fifty civilians, while Fowler caused one woman, Phuong, to suffer the loss of her loved one:

> Perhaps she would never know security: what right had I to value her less than the dead bodies in the square? Suffering is not increased by numbers: one body can contain all the suffering the world can feel. I had judged like a journalist in terms of quantity and I had betrayed my own principles; I had become as *engagé* as Pyle, and it seemed to me that no decision would ever be simple again. ([1955] 1973, 205)

Fowler, in short, has been just as complacently ignorant as Pyle. Each, in turn, has tried to become a political authority, attempting to force abstract principles on other human beings, instead of living a concrete moral existence himself. Yet each, meanwhile, has apparently maintained the best of intentions. Both characters, then, have been attacked, both defended; the resulting ambiguity is the fictional equivalent of the confusion that occurs with Kierkegaard's use of the same method. The technique produces a plethora of responses, as the conflicting criticism demonstrates. It is not necessary for the reader to solve the interpretive crux, however, for in Kierkegaard's mode of indirect communication, the author's own position is the least relevant. The ambiguity is intended to incite readers to examine their own positions, for an external theory is less meaningful than appropriation of the theory into one's own life. To accomplish this goal, Kierkegaard asserts repeatedly in his canon, a psychological and spiritual sobriety is required:

> Spiritually understood, to be sober requires first and foremost the completely and thoroughly reflected withdrawal of oneself as a single individual before God, alone before God; and then the pure expression of the ethical and what is ethically crucial—a clear and thoroughly worked out consciousness of one's own actual situation. (Kierkegaard 1967–78, 2:2034)

But this inward movement is not merely thought; it constitutes an ethical/religious *action* that is the real polemic behind the political works of both Kierkegaard and Greene. In *The Quiet American,* it is one action that never happens because, Greene intimates, both Pyle and Fowler fail to examine themselves. Instead, they blindly rely on external principles of other authorities: Pyle on the abstractions of York Harding, Fowler on the group principles of neutrality. Lacking the Kierkegaardian inwardness, neither becomes a real individual, neither understands the consequences of his complacency until the resulting situation soars out of control. The most glaring attack in the book, therefore, is not directed at American "interference" or British "noninvolvement" in Vietnam; far from partisan theories on the role of particular nations, Greene's real assault is aimed at self-deception, or as Kierkegaard calls it, "illusion" ([1944a] 1968, 28), the complacent assumption that acting in accordance with certain group rules is all that is required of a human being.

While Greene thus presents the external political situation as a backdrop in the novel, his larger concern seems to rest with the individual's reaction to that disjunctive situation. Touching the same issue, Stephen Spender's analysis of the poet's relationship to politics seems also to apply to Greene's position as novelist and communicator. Viewing the individual as "faced by an unprecedented crisis in the history of civilization, and with far-reaching public calamities," Spender asserts that "it is precisely within the consciousness of many separate individuals that the political struggle is taking place" (1978, 129). Greene defends those individuals by sympathizing with their apparent good intentions and by presenting so graphically the immensity of the external difficulties they need to overcome. But these problems, it is important to note, cannot be solved through the adoption of any theory found in Greene's book. For unlike propagandist writers who, in effect, try to become authorities by imposing their own theories on the group, Greene, like Kierkegaard, effaces himself in his position of communicator, leaving the reader free to construct a personal solution. Also unlike the more direct revolutionary writers (see the essays in White and Newman 1972), both Greene and Kierkegaard thus imply that literature achieves social importance as a means to personal change rather than national or large-group reform.

This repeated emphasis on the individual, together with that individual's concrete interpersonal relationships, emerges from the attack/defense method in *The Honorary Consul*. Centered on the various guises of the father image that haunts nearly every character in the book, the novel examines both the negative and the positive aspects of the concept, applying it not only to the familial father but also to church, state, small revolutionary group, or any other type of authority. The characters' conflicting responses to these extended father images may be similar to the reactions of readers and may therefore cause them to examine their own position with regard to external authority.

Set in a small town in Argentina, the novel opens with its central character, Dr. Eduardo Plarr, ruminating on his own absent father, who, involved somehow in the Paraguayan political situation, had left Eduardo and his mother fifteen years before, communicating with them only once during that time. Although, "at fourteen, [Eduardo] could not understand the motives which had made his father stay behind on the quay" ([1973] 1980, 10), as an adult, the son reasons that perhaps his father "in his foreign way was trying to imitate *machismo* when [despite his wife's protests] he chose to face alone the daily increasing dangers on the other side of the Paraguayan border, but it was only the stiff lip which showed upon the quay." Machismo, the third-person narrator explains, is a "sense of masculine pride" (p. 11). Plarr's conception of his father, as it arises from this description, is that of a proud, uncommunicative, distant, and possibly heroic figure who makes and executes the rules, a composite similar to the traditional father symbol, which suggests "power," "dominion," and "the world of moral commandments and prohibitions" (Cirlot 1962, 98). The image also parallels those "noble and uncommunicative characters" whom Doctor Plarr meets in Saavedra's novels but who "seemed to him too simple and too heroic ever to have had living models" (Greene [1973] 1980, 14). While the difference between image and existence appears easy for Plarr to recognize in the case of literature, through most of the novel he cannot or at least does not distinguish between the traditional symbol of fatherhood and his own father as a real man who may have had emotions and weaknesses behind the "stiff lip."

Having unwittingly fathered a child himself by Charley Fortnum's wife, Clara, Plarr maintains a posture of distance and apparent noninterest toward the unborn baby. In addition, he replays with Clara the external role that he saw his own father adopt toward his mother, communicating no emotion to his mistress and even becoming angry when she reveals feeling for him; he tells her nothing about his political activities and leaves her whenever he sees fit. More positively, but still never deviating from what he apparently perceives as the role model of fatherhood, he provides physical protection as her doctor and imitates sustenance by buying her a gift (a pair of sunglasses). Plarr becomes a mere image of himself (as he sees through the glasses); even his sexual consummation with Clara has been based on an idea: "I never really desired her, he thought, I only desired my idea of her" ([1973] 1980, 99). Plarr dramatizes fictionally, in other words, the Kierkegaardian figure of Johannes Climacus, who, in *Concluding Unscientific Postscript*, represents idea without its corresponding existential reality. Greene therefore does not ironize Plarr the man, for the man gives only a hint of his existence when he feels jealous of Charley's real love for Clara; instead, Greene attacks Plarr as empty image, fatherhood as a mere myth of itself.

In contrast to Plarr, León Rivas in one sense seems a mouthpiece for Greene's attack on the barren paternal image. A former priest, León had become disenchanted with an ecclesiastical authority grown too comfortable and distant from the real problems of the people.

> "[The Gospels] make no sense," the ex-priest said, "anyway not in Paraguay. 'Sell all and give to the poor'—I had to read that out to them while the old Archbishop we had in those days was eating a fine fish from Iguazú and drinking a French wine with the General . . . the children sat in the front rows with their pot bellies and their navels sticking out like doorknobs." ([1973] 1980, 143-44)

In the seminary, Rivas continues, "the Fathers . . . never touched on the horror . . . they saw no problem. They just sat comfortably down in the presence of the horror" (pp. 283-84). His professor of moral theology was "a man so cut and dried and sure of the truth. . . . You learn the rules and find they don't apply to any human case" (p. 274). Echoing Kierkegaard's anger at official behavior in the Danish Lutheran church, León's protests against what he viewed as a complacent Catholic establishment also coincide with his objection to his own father's practice: "He was a good *abogado*, but he never worked for a poor client. He served the rich faithfully until he died, and everyone said he was a good father because he left plenty of cash behind him" (p. 272).

But while Greene, like Kierkegaard, presents the disjunctive political condition through León's protests, the novelist (again like his predecessor) is probably more interested in the individual's reaction to that situation. On that score León, defended by the author for his views on paternal complacency, now comes under attack himself. For according to his own standard, one should not serve an establishment that ignores existential reality. Yet El Tigre, the all too distant leader of León's revolutionary group, seems the epitome of paternalistic abstraction coupled with official complacency. The man "who gives the orders" ([1973] 1980, 130), he does not involve himself with executing them: "After we announced the kidnapping all contact [with El Tigre] was broken" (p. 227). Realizing their inability to communicate with their leader, Aquino pinpoints the discrepancy between the image and the reality, recalling, ironically, Rivas's complaint against the archbishop: "[El Tigre] is somewhere in safety eating well and drinking well. He was not at the police station either when you rescued me. Is he never going to risk his own life like he risks ours?" (p. 252).

So while León had become angry in reaction to his perception of disjunction in the church, he serves hypocritical authority blindly as a member of the revolutionists; he has merely shifted his allegiance from one empty father image to another. In fact, he has stumbled into the same kind of duplicitous role-playing himself: he purports to be saving lives and helping people, yet he causes emotional suffering, is indirectly responsible for the death of Plarr, and comes dangerously close to killing Charley Fortnum, an innocent man involved in the plot only because the kidnappers had falsely identified him as the American ambassador. Mistaken identity, Greene seems to indicate, may be León's most serious problem. In an unusually intrusive observation, the third-person narrator refers to another of León's "identities": "[Charley Fortnum] interjected 'Father' as often as he could: it was somehow reassuring. A father didn't usually kill his son, although of course it had been a near miss in the case of Abraham" ([1973] 1980, 145). The apparently irreverent allusion is to the biblical story of Abraham and Isaac, in which Abraham is asked to sacrifice his son in order to show obedience to God. But when Abraham is about to kill Isaac, God spares the son's life. In Greene's novel, the passage is apparently not free indirect speech, since Charley is a serious man who does not speak jocosely. If Greene permits his narrator to intrude so untypically, then the purpose must be important: León, perhaps, has mistakenly identified himself as an Abraham figure—another abstraction—and thinks he has been called upon to "sacrifice" Charley Fortnum.

In *Fear and Trembling,* however, Kierkegaard addresses this very problem of Abraham's morality and explains that the act of killing Isaac would be ethically wrong yet religiously correct—but only because of the absolute nature of the individual's relationship with God (1983a, 73). The command to León, notably, comes not from God but from El Tigre; Rivas evidently confuses absolute obedience to God as final authority with limited obedience to a temporal father figure. In the process, law itself (an abstraction) becomes absolute instead of God (the Absolute Individual). León is not, therefore, a true Abraham, but rather another Climacus-figure limited to idea, like Doctor Plarr.

But Greene ultimately defends his priest, too, as he does so many of his other error-prone characters (for example, Querry in *A Burnt-Out Case,* even the whiskey priest in *The Power and the Glory*). Near the end of the novel, León sheds his image and acts as the real father that Charley Fortnum had hoped for and that Marta, León's wife, had continually believed in. As Plarr lies wounded outside the cottage, León disobeys El Tigre's orders: "The voice which [Plarr] now knew must be León's said, 'I heard the shot. I had to come . . . I could not kill a mouse'" ([1973] 1980, 315). And by addressing God as "Father" when asking his forgiveness, León confirms the belief in the possibility of a real, benevolent, loving, personal type of father who listens to one's plea; Father Rivas becomes such a person himself because, Greene implies, he acts as an individual instead of blindly as a member of a group and because he admits his past mistakes. The movement is essentially Kierkegaardian, for as the *Attack upon "Christendom"* makes clear, "in that way truth would enter the Establishment after all: [the Establishment] defends itself by condemning itself . . . has recourse to grace" ([1944a] 1968, 54).

Charley Fortnum, unlike Rivas, never really functioned as part of the Establishment. The characters repeatedly emphasize the fact that he is only an *honorary* consul with no real political importance to anyone. And the truth of the assertion seems only too clear when no one comes forward to negotiate for his release. Yet Charley, though weak enough to escape into alcoholic stupor at times, is by everyone's account the most praiseworthy "father" and husband in the novel. The rules associated with mythical fatherhood never occur to him; he is interested only in a real human relationship. He already loves and feels responsibility for the unborn child, even after discovering that the baby is not his own; he truly loves Clara, silently forgives her for her affair with Plarr, and shows heroic compassion when he decides to name the baby "Eduardo." While the other major characters thus react to the political chaos with cynicism, irony, and a blind attachment to unexamined, external, traditional, or revolutionary rules, Charley responds more personally by, in Kierkegaard's words, "existing as a Christian" (1968a, 34).

True social reform, both Kierkegaard and Greene imply, begins with the individual's externalization of inwardness. Kierkegaard articulates the process more specifically in *Works of Love:* "This hidden life of love is knowable *by its fruits*" (1962b, 28). The last phrase may be the most important one in both artists' credo, for it indicates that the inwardness, translated into love, "is an *act*—not an expression about, not a theoretical *conception*" (p. 182). Because Charley *acts* lovingly and caringly instead of merely theorizing about helping people as Rivas and Plarr do for most of the book, in Plarr's words, "Poor drunken Charley Fortnum wins the game" (Greene [1973] 1980, 313).

By attacking a strong but empty role model and yet defending an imperfect but living reality, Greene, I think, tries to confuse and thereby to stimulate the reader into an existential crisis. With Kierkegaard, the novelist asks first for self-examination and then for ethical action, for a shift from the theoretical into the existential. Like Kierkegaard's intention in *Attack upon "Christendom,"* therefore, Greene's purpose is only superficially negative: he attempts not to eliminate authority or the organization but to cleanse it by asking each individual member to look inward and condemn his or her own failures. For Greene, as for many other Christian artists, social reform begins with personal redemption; freedom from slavery is liberation from self-deception, a release from the imprisonment of attempting to exist as an abstraction. In his political works, as in his religious novels, Greene, unlike most contemporary novelists, thus demonstrates a Kierkegaardian faith in the power of the individual to perform a single moral act in response to the often bloody power struggles that serve as metaphorical illustrations of contemporary chaos in these books. In the epigraph to *The Honorary Consul*, the novelist uses Thomas Hardy's lines to state one cause of the modern social problem: "All things merge into one another—good into evil, generosity into justice, religion into politics." In the book, Greene implies a political solution that is itself revolutionary because it turns the lines upside down, aiming the writing backward into itself: the individual, he insists—not polemically but metaphorically—must change evil into good, justice into generosity, and politics into religion.

4

Toward an Actual Self: A Theory of Characterization

"In or about December, 1910," Virginia Woolf once quipped to a Cambridge audience, "human character changed" ([1924] 1950, 91). Her teasing remark gained widespread recognition, heralding for critics the shift "from one age of English literature to the next" (p. 103). But how, precisely, had character actually changed? To answer the question, Woolf narrated her journey in a carriage with a character she called "Mrs. Brown" and explained that the "Edwardians" (Wells, Bennett, Galsworthy) would present the elderly woman by describing the external social or physical details surrounding her, while the "Georgians" (Forster, Lawrence, Strachey, Joyce, Eliot) would attempt to reveal Mrs. Brown's internal "reality"—her thoughts, her motives, and, perhaps, her unconscious mind. The lady herself, Woolf insisted, remained the same: "Mrs. Brown is eternal, Mrs. Brown is human nature, Mrs. Brown changes only on the surface, it is the novelists who get in and out" (p. 103). The statement seems to suggest, among other things, that throughout the nearly three centuries of the novel's existence as a literary genre, writers of fiction, often as a group, have chosen to emphasize very different aspects of human beings who, according to Woolf, remain somehow essentially unchanged. This kernel of immutability that she posits is similar to what many philosophers have defined, traditionally, as the "self."

In recent decades, studies undertaken to describe approaches to character portrayal in the different literary eras have often included discussions about the "self" or the "essence" or the "identity" of a particular character. Examining eighteenth-century attitudes, for example, Patrick Coleman notes that era's predilection for thinking of characterization as "the discrimination of an object's peculiar essence" (1983, 52). During that century, this critic asserts, the "decline of plot" evident in such works as Sterne's *Tristram Shandy* and Diderot's *Jacques le fataliste* awarded to character, or "human agency," a "new significance" (p. 59). With the exception of such futuristic innovators, however, the precise locus of the essence is rarely questioned in eighteenth-century fiction. The self, in other words, is simply assumed by most novelists to exist and to be sufficiently important to warrant the author's interest.

In most major novels written during the nineteenth century, attention given to characterization continued to increase; the notion of a stable ego persisted[1] and was enhanced by its new thematic status in the bildungsroman, a genre that dealt directly with what W. J. Harvey calls "the search for identity" (1965, 120). In the Victorian novel, this identity, or self, was not only stable but was also "discrete, isolate, unique" (p. 119). Shirley Letwin concurs in this analysis of the nineteenth-century presentation of human agency, pointing out also that "a personal consciousness is understood [by the Victorians] to have a distinctive ordering and this is what constitutes a 'character'" (1983, 1447). Stability and uniqueness do not preclude change, however. Particularly for such writers in the moral tradition as Hawthorne, Dickens, Eliot, Dostoevsky, change or development (usually interpreted as moral or psychological "improvement") does occur, typically manifesting itself in new behavioral or social patterns.[2] But behavioral change, according to Harvey, "is still reconciled to the idea of a stable ego; one's identity lies precisely in the unique pattern of past changes which constitute one's individuality" (1965, 120). The locus and, more important, the constitution of this essential self, however, remain generally unexamined in this period either by the novelists or by the critics.

As fiction moves into the twentieth century, Virginia Woolf's perception of the changing methods of characterization become more strikingly relevant to the philosophical concept of the self. While the moderns, like the Victorians (or like Woolf's "Edwardians"), often view their characters externally in a given physical, economic, social, or moral context, the issue for earlier twentieth-century novelists "is not morality or society itself. It is rather the question of the [essential] self, of its very nature and constituents. The moderns seek to evoke and define what it is in people that shapes and informs the surfaces they present to the world, and the moral identity, such as it is, that they possess" (Hochman 1983, 136). No longer a stable, unexamined, purely socially manifested entity, the self, in such writers as Lawrence, Forster, Conrad, Joyce, Woolf, Proust, Mann, and Kafka, slips tauntingly into and out of view, now on the surface (later Woolf), now somewhere deeply entombed in the unconscious mind (later Joyce), often a psychological entity, sometimes a moral one, not always a controllable one. Busily defining and locating the self, though, the moderns still generally assumed its existence and diligently pursued its conscious realization. Character, against a background of professional and social interest in Freud's studies of personality, thus reached an apex of importance during the first half of the twentieth century. Behind this interest, of course, lay the mimetic assumption: the belief that a close correspondence existed between the selves of fictional characters and those of "real" people.

Soon after midcentury, however, the 250-year-old edifice of traditional character portrayal, painstakingly erected, exploded to reveal an apparent void where the structure of the self had been. Novelists, perhaps most clearly in America but certainly elsewhere as well, now seemed to believe that fictional characters did not represent "real" beings, did not "*re-produce* a pre-existing meaning" (Federman 1981b, 8). In almost defiant contrast to the traditional presentation of character that implies some kind of self, whether stable or fluid, the new fictional creatures seem to be composed entirely out of language. The novelist, Virginia Woolf would probably say, has left Mrs. Brown's carriage altogether and cannot even be sure of its (or her) existence. Federman describes the purely grammatical beings of postmodernist fiction:

> The people of fiction, the fictitious beings, will . . . no longer be well-made characters who carry with them a fixed identity, a stable set of social and psychological attributes—a name, a situation, a profession, a condition, etc. The creatures of the new fiction will be as changeable, as unstable, as illusory, as nameless, as unnamable, as fraudulent, as unpredictable as the discourse that makes them. . . . they will not appear to be simply what they are; they will be what they are: word-beings. (1981b, 13)

Such a "word-being," Federman implies, completely lacks a structure or self; it will be "made of fragments" and will remain "irrational, irresponsible, irrepressive, amoral, and unconcerned with the real world." The word-being, with the author and the reader, will "participate . . . in the creation of the fiction" (p. 13). The self, previously thought to be real, has become fiction while only language itself, according to Federman, can now be considered real (1981a, 303).

Reacting to this overthrow of mimeticism and the radical transition in methods of characterization, some critics, such as Gérard Genette, merely observe, as objectively as possible, "that the classical attributes of 'character' . . . have disappeared"; using Borges as a representative instance, Genette notes, again nonjudgmentally, that contemporary fiction "does *not accept person*" (1980, 247). Many recent critics, though—Arnold Weinstein and Raymond Federman are notable examples—seem to have adopted the same standpoint as the novelists regarding philosophy of characterization.[3] Thus, Weinstein calls the self "a supreme fiction" if a "necessary" one (1981, 7); he asserts further, in apparent agreement with Federman, that "it may be only out of language that a self can be made" (p. 17). Behind the fictional method or the critical commentary on characterization, in other words, the author's ideology reveals itself.

Of course, ideological concerns are hardly original with contemporary fiction. Although Woolf chose to ignore the subject in her

"Mrs. Brown" lecture, concentrating instead on literary technique, the assumptions of most novelists (including Woolf) from the eighteenth to the mid-twentieth century regarding the existence of a self (of whatever kind) reflect these novelists' belief in some sort of nonmaterial entity. In postmodern fiction, by contrast, the demise of fictional personhood and the linguistic reflexivity of so many contemporary novels indicate the absence of a belief in any type of "objective" reality.

In the study of Greene's fiction, then, we must ask how this author, as a Christian, existential novelist, can fit into this historical sketch with his techniques of characterization and his implied attitudes toward the self. The answer, not surprisingly, is far from simple, particularly since Greene's fictional canon stretches at this writing from 1929 to the mid-1980s, or from the period of high modernism well into the postmodern era, and since his techniques of characterization seem to span those evident from the eighteenth century to the present day. More specifically, although Greene is intensely concerned with character, he is also—perhaps more like novelists of earlier centuries—quite fond of plot, viewed as a series of incidents or adventures, which (in some of the minor novels, at least) sometimes captures the reader's interest more than a character does. Greene retains, moreover, a strong moral sense, and his characters pursue their ethical/psychological identities in ways that recall the flavor of the Victorian bildungsroman. Yet, with the modernists, he implies unconscious motives and tries to define the self; like the postmodernists, Greene can also create an apparent nonperson, and he can emphasize in his fiction the heavily subjective element of human perception. It may be useful, therefore, in the surplus of possibilities, to seek once again the aid of any relevant Kierkegaardian philosophical/religious principles concerning the identity of a human being.

In *Sickness unto Death* and in *Repetition*, Kierkegaard unfolds a theory of the self which I believe lies behind many of Greene's techniques of characterization. A study of the latter's use of this theory, therefore, can help to define his position in the chronology of fiction. Purportedly written by Anti-Climacus, another of Kierkegaard's pseudonymous authors, *Sickness unto Death* is not really a pseudonymous work, or at least not in the same sense as a work such as *Either/Or*, which intends to communicate only indirectly. As Walter Lowrie states in the translator's introduction, "These later works were the sincerest expression of [Kierkegaard's] own belief, and he had expected to publish them under his own name. The pseudonym was an afterthought" ([1941] 1954, 138). Why, then, did he bother to use a pseudonym at all? Probably, Lowrie answers, to assuage a feeling of guilt because the author, without authority, was offering to Christendom what he thought was a badly needed prescription for the perfection of Christianity (pp. 137–38). *Sickness unto Death*, therefore, can be taken literally, with Anti-Climacus functioning as a kind of antidote to Johannes Climacus in *Concluding Unscientific Postscript*. While the latter demonstrates ironically how one can reflect intensively and extensively *about* Christianity without, however, existing in it, the former offers the individual a way to actualize his or her Christianity: by eradicating all taint of despair in the personality, thereby becoming a true self.

Though writing in the mid-nineteenth century, Kierkegaard did not, like many British Victorians, view the self as a physical or psychological structure only. Certainly, it was partially that, as the subtitle to *Sickness unto Death* assumes ("A Christian Psychological Exposition for Edification and Awakening"). But for Kierkegaard, a human being possesses, most essentially, a spiritual component: "Man is spirit. But what is spirit? Spirit is the self" ([1941] 1954, 146). Continuing, he defines the self: "But what is the self? The self is a relation which relates itself to its own self, or it is that in the relation [which accounts for it] that the relation relates itself to its own self; the self is not the relation but [consists in the fact] that the relation relates itself to its own self" (p. 146; translator's interpolations). The passage emphasizes the self less as an object than as an activity. According to Mark Taylor, Kierkegaard, like Hegel in this case, views self as a "dynamic *process* by which potentialities are actualized" (1975, 115; italics mine). But the possibilities cannot even begin to actualize, Kierkegaard explains, unless all the composite parts of the individual are first accepted as a basis for a relationship:

> Man is a synthesis of the infinite and the finite, of the temporal and the eternal, of freedom and necessity, in short it is a synthesis. A synthesis is a relation between two factors. So regarded, man is not yet a self.
> In the relation between two, the relation is the third term as a negative unity, and the two relate themselves to the relation, and in the relation to the relation; such a relation is that between soul and body, when man is regarded as soul. ([1941] 1954, 146)

Rendered graphically, the first step toward selfhood might have the appearance of a single, horizontal or lateral connection between body and soul.[4]

body •→————————←• soul

But the second step, for Kierkegaard the most crucial (see 1967–78, 4:3902), must include an external, transcendent relationship.

> If on the contrary the relation relates itself to its own self, the relation is then the positive third term, and this is the self. . . .
> A derived, constituted, relation is the human self, a relation which relates itself to its own self, and in relating itself to its own self relates itself to another. ([1941] 1954, 146)

The diagrammatic representation shifts in the new relationship to allow for a vertical as well as a horizontal movement and thus creates a triangular structure to replace the single linear one, with the arrows again denoting the constant activity involved:

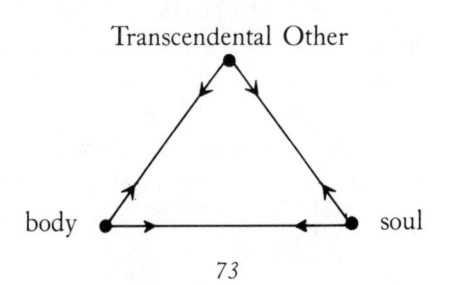

```
            Transcendental Other
                    •
                   ↗ ↖
                  /   \
                 /     \
                /       \
         body •→—————←• soul
```

The Kierkegaardian self, then, unlike eighteenth-century and many nineteenth-century ideas of personhood, is not a static entity, or even a static entity merged with a mobile one; on the contrary, the self, "every instant it exists, is in process of becoming" ([1941] 1954, 163). It must be continually reiterated, during every new moment, or the individual loses the relationship, stagnates, and falls into despair, which Kierkegaard defines as "the disrelationship in a relation that relates itself to itself" (p. 148).

Antithetical to the self, despair, according to Kierkegaard, is a universal sickness ([1941] 1954, 155–61) that, if allowed to progress unchecked, is self-consuming yet can never entirely destroy itself (p. 150). Despair is "to die and yet not to die . . . to live to experience death" (p. 151), a sickness *unto* death, without the relief of actual, physical death.[5] The despair that taints every human being, Kierkegaard insists, is "sin" (p. 208–13). But he denies that his view of universal sickness and sin is a "depressing" one: "On the contrary it is uplifting, since it views every man in the aspect of the highest demand made upon him, that he be spirit" (p. 155). His optimism also rests, perhaps, on his vision of a possible cure from sickness and sinfulness: "the opposite of being in despair is believing" (p. 182); "the opposite of sin is not virtue but faith" (p. 213). And even if no human being is capable of an absolute or sustained belief, Kierkegaard says, anyone can strive toward the ultimate goal of faith; the process of striving opens the individual to the establishment of a self which may begin only with the aid of the transcendent Being. "Belief" and "self," then, merge in Kierkegaardian ideology.

In the aesthetic works, this theory of self-becoming appears to dominate Kierkegaard's methodology of characterization. His fictional beings, in fact, might even be classified according to whether or how they demonstrate any self-activity, or awareness of themselves as spirit united with a transcendent Being. Certainly, the narrator of "Diapsalmata" in the first volume of *Either/Or* apparently lacks this consciousness and manifests the despair that Kierkegaard describes in *Sickness unto Death*.[6] Generally, the narrator maintains a vision that seems almost entirely negative: "This life is topsy-turvy and terrible, not to be endured. . . . My view of life is utterly meaningless. . . . Life has become a bitter drink to me, and yet I must take it like medicine, slowly, drop by drop" (1971, 1:24–25). Of course, the negative pole in Kierkegaard's concept of mobile irony is both common and even necessary for most individuals. The objectionable stance, he maintains, is not the negativity as part of an eventual swing toward positivity but the negativity in isolation, a view—more common in the postmodernists—that eliminates the possibility of spirit and results in an almost total void where the self would be. In "Diapsalmata," the narrator expresses the state symbolically, using, as the translators explain in an endnote, very inconspicuous signs from Hebrew grammar to indicate his utter insignificance: "I am as shrunken as a Hebrew *shewa*, weak and silent as a *daghesh lene;* I feel like a letter printed backwards in the line, and yet as ungovernable as a three-tailed Pasha, as jealous for myself and my thoughts as a bank for its notes, and as generally introverted as any *pronomen reflexivum*" (1:22).

The obsessive introversion, a characteristic escape mechanism of much modernist literature, leads paradoxically to a weaker rather than a stronger sense of self, according to Kierkegaard, for such introversion is merely a psychological phenomenon, lacking any spiritual component. But in spite of the emptiness, the desire for that self apparently is not lost: "How barren is my soul and thought, and yet forever tortured by empty birthpangs, sensual and tormenting! Must my spirit then ever remain tongue-tied, must I always babble?" (1971, 1:23) This narrator, interestingly, would find many counterparts to himself in Kierkegaard's "Shadowgraphs" and in the postmodernist fiction of artists such as Beckett or Barthelme. But whereas characters in the contemporary novels seem intended to demonstrate that self is merely another illusion, Kierkegaard's portraits of apparent emptiness, as I have shown in earlier chapters, represent only one type of existential possibility, which is pitted against a different sort in the companion volume of *Either/Or* (Judge William) and in *Stages on Life's Way* (Quidam).

In "Quidam's Diary," to cite only one example, Quidam, like the narrator in "Diapsalmata," seems acutely aware of his own negative attitude toward existence: "Melancholy is my very nature" (1940, 188). Even the move toward repentance, as Frater Taciturnus points out in a later chapter of the work, is "not a positive movement out to or on till, but a negative movement in at, not a doing but a letting something befall one" (p. 430). Yet, in spite of the pervasive negativity, Quidam's attempts to choose "the religious" (p. 211) throughout the diary lead him to a strong, if tortured, belief: "Eternity will . . . heal all sickness" (p. 356). An awareness of personal guilt, together with a continual struggle to believe, forms, in the Kierkegaardian fictional character who has attained such a plateau, the basis of a transcendental relationship that the author views as integral selfhood, not only of a fictional character, but also of a human being.

Greene's theory of characterization, also mimetically based, seems to rest on a similar ideology of essential selfhood. Presenting both negative and positive examples of existential possibilities, he treats fictional characters as though they were real people and tends to view each one as a potential self manifesting a "paradigm of traits" (Chatman 1978, 126) which the reader may use to determine whether that self is being actualized.

Two representative negative approaches to a study of the self are *The Heart of the Matter* and *The Comedians*. The former, published in 1948, is one of the author's early studies of suicide.[7] Set in the grim, oppressive surroundings of hot and humid West Africa, the novel highlights the overwhelming problems of self-definition in Henry Scobie, a police officer who, with his dissatisfied, "intellectual" wife, Louise, seems trapped by the sterile and corrupt environment. Greene presents his protagonist as a system of apparent virtues which Scobie himself has constructed to describe what he thinks are the motives behind his actions.[8]

One of the most obvious of these traits, mentioned repeatedly, is Scobie's apparent sense of responsibility: "It had always been his responsibility to maintain happiness in those he loved" ([1948]

1971, 19); "his wife's absence was like a garrulous companion in the room reminding him of his responsibility" (p. 15); "there was something he had to do, someone he had to save" (p. 99); "he had sworn to preserve Louise's happiness, and now he had accepted another and contradictory responsibility" (p. 186); "if only, he thought, I could so manage that she never suffers again, but he knew that he had set himself an impossible task" (p. 247). Significantly, though, such "responsibility," which is usually an ethical asset, as Judge William recognizes in *Either/Or*,[9] leaves Scobie with an "odd premonitory sense of guilt" (p. 9).

As the novel progresses, the reader may gradually become aware of a deeper problem from which the guilt stems: Scobie is not nearly so responsible as he thinks he is, for his habit of accountability toward others, Greene indicates, does not apply to himself. Addressing God, for example, Scobie refuses to accept responsibility for his own behavior: "Take your sponge of gall. You made me what I am" ([1948] 1971, 263). Moreover, by his passive consent, Scobie allows Yusef's men to perform the actual murder of Ali, thereby relieving Scobie himself of the responsibility for the physical act. The paradoxical behavior reveals the flaw in what turns out to be the character's false sense of responsibility toward others—particularly women—in his life and serves to demonstrate an important aspect of Greene's trait-building theory of characterization. According to the author, a trait cannot be defined as positive merely by viewing it in abstraction. That is, the idea of a virtue, falsely applied, may not only cease to be virtue but may actually become sin. In Scobie's case, an exaggerated responsibility directed exclusively toward human beings shifts subtly into a proud desire to control other people's lives, perhaps to achieve potency in an otherwise impotent existence.

Interestingly, Kierkegaard's Quidam, in *Stages on Life's Way*, also wrestles with the problem of responsibility. After courting a girl, Quidam realizes that he cannot reconcile marrying an essentially nonreligious, or aesthetic person with what he feels is his own calling to a religious existence. And worse, now that the girl has become interested in him, he feels responsible for her welfare, even to the extent of wondering whether she could "become insane" (1940, 251) over her loss of him; he therefore plans to act like a scoundrel so that she will, instead, be glad of a deliverance from his false love. But while the diary recounts Quidam's six-month-long obsession "over his unhappy responsibility," it also reveals his belief that this burden of accountability to a human being places him "on unhappy terms with the eternal meaning of life" (p. 250). Ultimately, having tried all in his power to help the girl without resorting to actual wrongdoing, he admits his guilt in making her unhappy, states that his punishment is the consciousness of that guilt, but hopes "that a merciful Governance [God] will in actuality make this punishment less by helping her" (p. 359).

While both Scobie and Quidam have borne responsibility, then, only Quidam, by trusting God, has actualized the trait; in Kierkegaard's theory, in other words, the character has accepted the relationship with God and thereby produced a true self. Thus, in Greene's method of characterization, an apparently positive trait may not always be taken at face value. In Kierkegaard's words, the character may have "embellished an aesthetic principle to make it look like an ethical principle" (1940, 428). More relevant to the characterization, then, is not the trait itself but the question of whether the trait leads to, or at least begins, the process of self-actualization which, in Kierkegaard's definition, must include the transcendent relationship.

The numerous references to Scobie's pity illustrate another apparently positive trait enclosing an empty shell. Often the allusions to pity occur in passages where Greene is using free indirect speech: "He [Scobie] couldn't describe to Mrs. Bowles the . . . terrible impotent feeling of . . . pity"; "if one knew, he wondered, the facts, would one have to feel pity even for the planets?" ([1948] 1971, 139). "Pity smoldered like decay at his heart. He would never rid himself of it. He knew from experience how passion died away and how love went, but pity always stayed. Nothing ever diminished pity. The conditions of life nurtured it. There was only a single person in the world who was unpitiable, oneself" (p. 205). The voices of both Greene and Scobie are evident in these passages which express the character's feeling through the author's images. And the diction ("impotent," "smoldered," "decay") indicates that neither Greene nor Scobie views pity as a positive trait. As in the author's negative use of apparent responsibility, therefore, pity becomes a vice that enables the character to disguise his desperate (if unconscious) attempt to feel superior through the external appearance of virtue.[10] For Scobie, accordingly, pity becomes a way to denigrate the value of others; significantly, he reduces the status of his wife and his mistress with epithets such as "poor Louise" (p. 12) or "poor you [Helen]" (p. 205); he frequently pities what he perceives as both women's ugliness. Unlike Quidam's reductions of the girl in his diary, however, Scobie's pity is not based upon the love that arises from the relationship with God.

To Scobie, in contrast, the manifestation of even a human love is, by his own admission, merely a habit, a series of patterns, another trait which, like his pity and responsibility, remains empty of positive content. Many if not most of this character's actions arise out of conformity to a pattern of behavior: "Life always repeated the same *pattern:* there was always, sooner or later, bad news that had to be broken, comforting lies to be uttered, pink gins to be consumed to keep misery away" ([1948] 1971, 222; italics mine). Keeping a diary was another empty habit: "He couldn't have told himself why he stored up this record . . . perhaps the reason was that forty years ago at a preparatory school he had been given a prize . . . for keeping a diary throughout one summer holiday, and the habit had simply stayed" (p. 128). Many of his religious practices were also merely routine: "It was the first Saturday of the month and he always went to Confession on that day. . . . the awful languor of routine fell on his spirits" (p. 175).

It is not surprising, therefore, to discover the same languor of the empty, external habit seeping into a human relationship to replace the love that is missing. Ready to greet Louise on her return from South Africa, he realizes the void: "His mouth felt stiff with welcome; he practised on his tongue phrases which would seem warm and unaffected, and he thought: what a long way I have travelled to make me rehearse a welcome" ([1948] 1971, 239). Later, he diagnoses his real problem by posing a question: "Do I in my heart of hearts, love either of them, or is it only that this automatic pity goes out to any human need—and makes it worse?" (p. 241). Finally, Wilson answers the question for him: "You don't love anybody except yourself, your dirty self" (p. 281). But the self to which Wilson refers is clearly not the actualized Kierkegaardian self. Rather, Scobie seems to love his own human ego, or only one portion of the interacting transcendental relationship that Kierkegaard requires of the actual self. For although Scobie thinks of God frequently enough, his actions, like the broken rosary beads he carries in his pocket, imply a disruption in the relationship; his apparent belief, together with his love, his pity, and his responsibility, has become a meaningless habit in his life. Even the word "self" becomes negative in the absence of the spiritual relationship.

In the Kierkegaardian framework described in *Sickness unto Death*, such a disruption constitutes despair. This kind of disrelationship becomes explicit in Greene's novel when Scobie begins to question God's authority: "Why didn't you let her drown?" ([1948] 1971, 142). Later, again in contrast to Kierkegaard's character Quidam, Scobie chooses a woman instead of God: "God can wait, he thought: how can one love God at the expense of one of his creatures?" (p. 217). Soon afterward, Scobie experiences the result of this choice: "There was no hope anywhere he turned his eyes: the dead figure of the God upon the Cross, the plaster Virgin, the hideous stations, representing a series of events that had happened a long time ago. It seemed to him that he had only left for his exploration the territory of despair" (p. 260). In the disrelationship, Greene asserts, the individual is divorced from God: "When he walked beside her [Louise] into the church it was as if he had entered this building for the first time—a stranger" (p. 261). God even becomes an "enemy" (p. 276) that one can "strike" (p. 287); Scobie watches him "bleed" (p. 279). Repeating the image of the broken rosary, now lost, Greene seems to indicate that for Scobie, who by his silence has caused the murder of Ali, the relationship with God has been severed: "Oh God, he thought, I've killed you: you've served me all these years and I've killed you at the end of them" (p. 291). Thus, Scobie alone performs the act of severance; he freely chooses to ignore the inner voice (of God); he decides to continue the disrelationship; and he, finally, "[turns] his back on the altar" (p. 306).

Equating the disruption of the relation between Scobie and God with the disintegration of the actual self, Greene uses metaphorical diction that recalls the shrunken Hebrew *shewa* of Kierkegaard's "Diapsalmata": "Home to him meant the reduction of things to a firm, friendly, unchanging minimum" ([1948] 1971, 14). Remaining insignificant through most of the story for lack of any spiritual nourishment, Scobie's actual self apparently disappears almost completely after he becomes estranged from God because of his role in the murder of Ali. Greene notes that the failing character "had no shape left, nothing you could touch and say: this is Scobie" (p. 289). And of course, the metaphorical violence to the spiritual self culminates for Scobie in the physical act of suicide, a way to "protect [Louise] from myself forever" (p. 311). The potentially spiritual self is never entirely absent, however, as Scobie's last words suggest, when he addresses the God he thought he had killed in himself.

If Scobie never actualized his potential self during his life, though, his character is nevertheless presented as essentially different from the postmodernist character who also seems to lack a self. Both types are empty vessels, creatures of pattern, systems of external traits, automatons apparently without moral substance like the characters of Beckett or Barthelme. But the difference lies in the ideology. While the postmodern character lacks an actual self because its creator believes any kind of self to be illusory, Greene's developed characters who have lost the self seem to have done so through their own free choice. Unlike the typical postmodern artist, Greene assumes in his characterization—more like the high modernist author—that a nonmaterial self can exist and be defined. But Greene's assumption diverges from modernism, too, because his definition of self includes a soul and an active relationship with God.

In the fictional world of the Christian, existential artist, therefore, a character like Scobie who fails to apply apparent belief to existence and who therefore manifests only theoretical, humanized traits is deliberately refusing to actualize his or her potential self.

Such a refusal constitutes the kind of living death that Kierkegaard describes in *Sickness unto Death*, which becomes clear in Greene's later, more complex, and possibly most negative study of the smothered self, *The Comedians*. If Scobie at least struggled against his awareness of spirituality, Brown, the middle-aged narrator of *The Comedians*, has withdrawn not only from spiritual awareness but from any type of positive belief as well. The result, from a technical, novelistic point of view, according to Greene, is a character composed almost entirely of an external mask and one who, resembling Federman's postmodern word-beings at least superficially, is highly conscious of personal hollowness and, indeed, even seems to revel in it.

As the title suggests, Greene uses the theatrical motif of the comic drama to present his self-less character. Early in the novel, Brown attempts to dismiss his entire life by categorizing it as a genre: he speaks of "the confused comedy of our lives" ([1966] 1976, 30); he insists that life is "a comedy, not the tragedy for which I have been prepared" and that we are all "driven by an authoritative practical joker towards the extreme point of comedy" (p. 31); later, he asserts that his mother was "an accomplished comedian" (p. 88) and that "we belonged to a world of comedy not of tragedy" (p. 198).

Paradoxically, however, he admits that he has not learned "the trick of laughter" ([1966] 1976, 185). His use of black humor, of course, can hardly qualify as comedy that evokes a positive attitude, for the dark humor is inherently disjunctive, carrying overtones of anger and cynicism. Reading a Haitian newspaper report, for example, Brown inserts his own funny but hostile interpretation:

> The Secretary for Education was announcing a six-year plan to eliminate illiteracy in the north—why the north in particular? No details were given. Perhaps he was depending on a satisfactory hurricane. Hurricane Hazel in '54 had eliminated a great deal of illiteracy in

the interior—the extent of the death-roll had never been disclosed. (P. 120)

And as the dead body of Joseph, Brown's faithful servant, is carried past him near the end of the book, the narrator maintains his mask of comic indifference but betrays a note of bitterness: "One of the men asked 'Do you know him?' 'Yes,' I said. 'He used to make good rum punches'" (p. 346).

Another element that belies the narrator's assertion of life as a comedy is the background of horrific Haitian violence that is anything but comic; Greene uses the setting, in fact, to indicate quite clearly the kind of reality that opposes Brown's protective stance. In the introduction to *The Comedians*, the author takes pains to announce to his readers that "Haiti really was the bad dream of the newspaper headlines" ([1966] 1976, xi). And Brown himself later makes similar statements: "Haiti was not an exception in a sane world: it was a small slice of everyday taken at random" (p. 158); "the nightmares are real in this place. . . . more real than ourselves" (p. 199); "the situation isn't abnormal. It belongs to human life" (pp. 199–200).

In addition to this emphasis on a worldview of chaos, Greene uses image patterns referring to Brown's personal status to indicate that the comic mask is merely a way of escape from responsible involvement. Yet, if that involvement may seem futile to the contemporary individual, the alternative to belief in ethical choice and action, Greene seems to imply through these image patterns, is the failure to produce an actualized self.

Lacking the particularity of a first name and uncertain even of the authenticity of his surname, Brown, in fact, suffers from a chronic identity crisis. His birth in Monte Carlo, the "city of transients" ([1966] 1976, 274), demonstrates the absence of national bonds: "I was born in Monaco. . . . That is almost the same as being a citizen of nowhere" (p. 287). At maturity, he found himself "without roots" (p. 345), or at least with roots that "would never go deep enough anywhere to make me a home" (p. 274).

Other images that imply a despairing rather than a positive comic view include numerous references to dryness, which may suggest Brown's lack of the dynamic fertilizing process that leads to a viable ethical or religious self. The narrator's frightening dream on the night of his mother's death indicates that Greene views the dryness as a negative image of this character; typically, Brown is a passive observer in his dream who assumes no personal responsibility for his own aridity.

> I was walking by the side of a lake in the moonlight and I was dressed like an altar-boy—I felt the magnetism of the still quiet water, so that every step I took was nearer to the verge, until the uppers of my black boots were submerged. Then a wind blew and the surge rose over the lake, like a small tidal wave, but instead of coming towards me, it went in the opposite direction, raising the water in a long retreat, so that I found I walked on dry pebbles and that the lake existed only as a gleam on the far horizon of the desert of small stones, which wounded me through a hole in my boots. I woke to an agitation that shook the stairs and floors. ([1966] 1976, 85)

Among all of the images contradicting the positive comic standpoint, however, the diction signifying morbidity indicates most devastatingly both a radically different viewpoint and, even more important, a failed self-actualization. The personification of the Kierkegaardian "living death," Brown seems to use the term "comedy" to mean something similar to the negative polar position in Kierkegaard's description of the ironic standpoint. Like any ironist who chooses to remain in such a position, Brown has completely withdrawn from enjoyment of or involvement in life. His vocabulary, indeed, contains continual references to the moribund. His obsession with locating his lost paperweight coffin, which he later discovers in the dead *ministre*'s pocket, is representative: "The small brass paper-weight shaped like a coffin, marked with the letters R.I.P., that I bought for myself one Christmas in Miami . . . had no value . . . but it was mine" ([1966] 1976, 56). His smiles, too, often include references to death: "We lay down in a shallow declivity under the palms like bodies given a common burial. . . . We—the uncoloured—were all of us too far away from home. I lay as inert as *Monsieur le Ministre*" (p. 198).

Greene seems to link these death images with Brown's lack of belief. He regards faith negatively as a temptation; he believes, literally, in nothing and even identifies himself with inanimate objects.

> The rootless have experienced, like all the others, the temptation of sharing the security of a religious creed or a political faith, and for some reason we have turned the temptation down. We are the faithless. . . . We have chosen nothing except to go on living, "rolled round on Earth's diurnal course, With rocks and stones and trees." ([1966] 1976, 345)

Greene offers these image patterns to help the reader construct the character. Like Scobie, Brown is presented as a paradigm of traits which, superficially regarded, appear in the former as morally positive and in the latter as ethically neutral; actually, for both characters the traits gradually emerge as negative concepts in the minds of many readers.

But with some other characters in *The Comedians*, the technique is reversed: an apparently negative or at least morally neutral trait is shown to be a mere construct of the narrator's perception and an overlay for a more positive trait that indicates self-actualization. H. J. Jones serves as one example of this method of characterization.

Manifesting what at first seems to be a similar approach to life's disjunction, Jones appears on numerous occasions also to be playing the role of the clown. He appeals to the other characters, to begin with, on the basis of his ability to make them laugh. When Brown questions Tin Tin about Jones's behavior, for example, she expresses her approval thus: "'Oh yes. I liked him. I liked him a lot.' 'What did you like so much?' 'He made me laugh,' she said" ([1966] 1976, 185). Martha comments similarly: "Darling, he makes us laugh" (p. 277). And Philipot also notices: "The men loved him. He made them laugh" (p. 347).

A second aspect of Jones's apparent role as the fool becomes evident through Greene's insertion of several farcical episodes in the story. One of these is Jones's suggestion to the *Medea*'s purser concerning the use of condoms to replace balloons at the ship's concert: "His [the purser's] desk was littered with great swollen phalluses.... 'Tomorrow is the ship's concert,' he explained to me, 'and we have no balloons. It was Mr. Jones's idea that we should use these.' I saw that he had decorated some of the sheaths with comic faces in coloured ink" ([1966] 1976, 29).

Another instance of Jones's involvement with farce arises when he leaves the *Medea* disguised in the female garb of a Spanish flamenco dancer, crowned with the headgear of a Vollendam peasant.

> The ship's sentry stared at us agape; he hadn't known there was a woman aboard, and such a woman, too. Jones, as he passed the sentry, gave him an appraising and provocative glance from his brown eyes.... At the foot of the gangway he embraced the purser and left him smudged on both cheeks with pre-shave powder. ([1966] 1976, 267)

But the comedy of these episodes, it is important to note, differs markedly from the black humor of Brown's observations. While Brown reflects negativity and bitterness in his lines, Jones views the comic situation as one of positive enjoyment. The opposition between the two views is crucial for purposes of self-development, for as Kierkegaard points out repeatedly in *Sickness unto Death*, a self cannot take shape in the pervading negativity of despair. Jones's self, Greene indicates, though difficult to locate, is by no means so completely stifled as Brown's.

Like Brown, Jones has no knowledge of a father and apparently no geographic roots, and along with the narrator, he deceives people into accepting his social mask in exchange for his real self. Unlike his fellow comedian, however, Jones seems to believe in what Kierkegaard views as a combination of possibility and necessity: the merging of the two yields a complete self (Kierkegaard [1941] 1954, 168).[11] Jones, then, apparently recognizing this need to strive, or "become," forges a beginning of the actualization process, while Brown remains a passive spectator, accepting neither necessity nor possibility. In the novel, Greene renders the latter concept imaginatively when Jones joins young Philipot's untrained and undersupplied forces to oppose, at incredible odds, the seemingly impregnable Haitian dictatorship. The attempt, of course, is an offense against reason, but it seems to imply a belief in a power beyond human logic. Of course, without the aid of authorial commentary in this first-person novel, the reader is free to judge such an act, as the narrator does, to be foolhardy, suicidal, and undertaken only to avoid the embarrassment of refusing to conform to the heroic image of himself which Jones had presented to Martha. But though Greene does not rule out the presence of these negative motives for Jones's acts, the implied author also includes subtle suggestions that the act does indicate an initiation into the search for an identity and that this very striving toward the establishment of a self constitutes the process of becoming one.

Perhaps the most vital clue to Jones's progress toward self-actualization is the link with one of Henry James's short fictions, "The Great Good Place." In the story—which Brown begins to read but typically fails to explore fully, mocking the author instead ([1966] 1976, 309)—the butler (whose name is also Brown) repeatedly reminds George Dane that Dane wears an external, imprisoning mask to conform to society's expectations. But though Dane desires to shed the mask in order to rediscover his true identity or self, his "Brother" verbalizes this wish for Dane and pinpoints the purpose of "the great good place": "I don't speak of the putting off of one's self; I speak only—if one has a self worth sixpence—of the getting it back" (James [1900] 1974, 2554).

Jones, like Dane, fails to articulate his wish precisely, but Greene clearly links the two characters through obvious references to the Jamesian story title: Jones, awakening briefly from his sleep while waiting for Philipot in the cemetery, remarks that "this was 'a good place'" (Greene [1966] 1976, 329); also, when recounting the story of Jones's death, Philipot tells Brown that Jones had "found what he called a good place" (p. 349). The latter's initials (H.J.), too, represent still another probable allusion to Henry James, many of whose characters devote their lives to a search for their identities. And finally, a description of the stone monument erected to commemorate Jones opens the novel; stone, traditionally, is an indication of self-formation. According to J. E. Cirlot, "Stone is a symbol of being, of cohesion and harmonious reconciliation with self. . . . The stone when whole symbolized unity and strength" (1962, 299).

Jones, therefore, with his symbolic attempts to "smell water" (symbolizing his concern for the inner life) and his insistence on carrying his cocktail case containing "spirits," is a character roughly similar to the Kierkegaardian image of one who, though certainly not overtly religious, at least begins the process of self-realization through a belief in ethical possibility made concrete through responsible action. In the construction of this character, Greene erects, with the help of the reader, a paradigm of negative traits mixed with positive ones; he assumes both the possibility and the actuality of the self. Crucially, he hints at the almost miraculous effect of pursuing it: even the decision to search for an integral self apparently has the power to change a negative paradigm into a cluster of more positive moral traits.

Mr. and Mrs. William Abel Smith are two other characters constructed from a similar type of negative/positive model. The naive but gentle and loving Americans, who arrive in Haiti with the sole intention of promoting economic and personal recovery through vegetarianism, may seem at first to be comically, even absurdly, ignorant of the disjunctive condition of the contemporary world. When they are forced to recognize chaos and evil, however, they respond quite differently than Brown does. Instead of withdrawing into passivity and negativity or into a view that is only theoretically "comic," they allow themselves to appear as comic figures in their assumption that an individual can deal effectively with chaos. The antithesis of the narrator's uninvolvement, the Smiths attempt ethical action by submerging themselves in the affairs of others. Beginning with Mrs. Smith's concern for Mr. Fernandez on the ship, images of active involvement continue with her interference in the management of Philipot's hearse, with their intervention in Jones's arrest, and, finally, with Mrs. Smith's seemingly incredible rescue of Brown from the hands of Concasseur. Their ability to interact effectively with others, Greene intimates, is the result of the nourishment they give to their ethical and spiritual identities: images of water (the filled swimming pool, for example) and of vegetative life surround the Smiths, in direct contrast to Brown's aridity and rootlessness.

If their eccentric commitment seems comical, however, it is also latently powerful (note that Mr. Smith's middle name is Abel), as evidenced by Mrs. Smith's triumph over Concasseur and by their ability to secure employment for Brown after he abandons his hotel. Undaunted by the defeat of their proposed vegetarian center in Haiti, they show renewed vigor by their fresh attempt in Santo Domingo. In addition, they are respected and liked by Jones and even by Brown, who finally acknowledges that he considers their idealism beautiful, even "heroic" ([1966] 1976, 237). According to Greene, then, the Smiths' unexamined belief is less harmful, more life-giving, and more self-actualizing than Brown's rationalized and completely negative unbelief, which results, indirectly, in the death of Jones and, if one can judge from the imagery, in Brown's own metaphoric death as well.

In view of the clusters of more positive traits that can be uncovered beneath the surface qualities of Jones and of the Smiths, Brown's negativity may begin to seem less and less creditable to the reader. The mask of comic indifference then becomes not humor but despair; in Kierkegaard's words, Brown's negativity would be conceived as "the sickness, not as the cure" ([1941] 1954, 143), for the modernist perception of disjunction. Hence, in the final analysis, the characterization of Brown, though it may seem quite as vacuous as any contemporary word-being, nevertheless diverges from the assumption of nothingness underlying postmodernism. Instead, Greene's character is based on an assumption of free choice (though, of course, the act of choice may be partially limited by ignorance, environment, etc.): unbelief causes Brown to choose total disengagement and to decide at every moment to attempt a fresh assault on his already moribund self. A more effective response, Greene implies through the development of other characters, would be to believe, as Kierkegaard does, that possibility can be actualized to produce a self which can effect change, even in a chaotic world. To return to Virginia Woolf's analogy, then, Greene produces his "Mrs. Brown" by studying external *and* internal traits and by pinpointing the discrepancy between them. By so doing, the Christian existential artist spans with his techniques the Edwardian, the Georgian, and even the postmodernist approaches to characterization, creating in his major characters a predominantly negative model with positivity imprisoned at its core.

Somewhat less eclectic in methodology and more positive in final result is Greene's essentially modernistic attempt to reach that core through his portrait of Querry in *A Burnt-Out Case*. Like Woolf's approach to Mrs. Brown, Greene's method, which he implements by means of the journey motif, is to probe more and more deeply the inner substance of the character in order to create a more valid cluster of traits. The progress toward interiority is gradual, of course, and the division between exterior and interior stages arbitrary. But in a general sense, Greene begins with Querry's external and conscious identity and proceeds slowly, with many regressions, toward the discovery of attitudes which, like those of Kurtz in Conrad's *Heart of Darkness* (which *A Burnt-Out Case* clearly resembles), Querry had at first not been aware of possessing.

The novel opens with a description of Querry's attitudes and actions while on the boat that will carry him to the leproserie. Designating the character simply as "the cabin passenger," Greene seems immediately to imply Querry's appearance of nonidentity during this stage of the trip. Impersonality permeates Querry's thinking: even when he mentions "feeling" he tends to rely on a reasoning process to establish an attitude, as is suggested by the parody of the Cartesian syllogism that opens the novel, "I feel discomfort, therefore I am alive," and by Querry's attempt to explain logically to the captain Christ's walking on water. Somewhat later, Greene reveals that Querry's rationalistic attitude extends to the whole question of God's existence. Querry has long ago concluded that the traditional, abstract theistic arguments can easily be demolished; he thinks that he has therefore adopted a standpoint of nonbelief and, in direct opposition to the Kierkegaardian view that considers despair as the modern malady, Querry regards belief as an irrational "sickness" ([1961] 1974, 21) to be avoided.

Querry's strong emphasis on cognitive processes extends also to his examining the motives for his actions. In discovering these motives, he believes that he has already plunged far beneath the surface, and he assumes, at least consciously, that he has reached the Conradian heart of darkness—the egoism in himself. Unveiling the weakness he despises, Querry articulates, for example, what he views as the selfishness of his artistic endeavors: "What I have built, I have always built for myself, not for the glory of God or the pleasure of a purchaser!" ([1961] 1974, 53).[12] Not only has he positioned himself foremost in importance, he tells Dr. Colin, but he has also completely failed to consider anyone else: "Your vocation is quite a different one, doctor. You are concerned with people. I wasn't concerned with the people who occupied my space—only with the space" (p. 45).

These apparent self-discoveries, which follow the modernistic method of delving into interiority, result for Querry in a response similar to that of Brown in *The Comedians:* like Kierkegaard's ironist at the negative pole, both characters defensively withdraw from the disjunction they perceive in society and in themselves. While Brown's protective effort results in an abstract theory of the world as absurdist comedy, Querry's reaction is an inability (or perhaps refusal) to feel; an emotional leper, he cannot suffer or experience pain. All of these attitudes, of course, represent the character's view of his own qualities at the beginning of his psychospiritual journey. But though Greene again seems to prompt the reader to construct a paradigm of traits for the "hero" of this novel, as Querry's journey continues, the reader may decide to reverse the model used for

Scobie and for Brown. Instead of an apparently positive or at least neutral paradigm that ultimately emerges as negative, Querry, like the Smiths, seems to embody a system of apparently negative traits that, when more deeply examined, reveals itself as only an outer shell which in turn is found to contain positive material. Querry's own parable about the multiple layers of eggs that he narrates to Marie Rycker suggests this model, as do the superior's cautionary statements to Doctor Colin: "If I begin to probe into what lies behind that desire to be of use, oh well, I might find some terrible things, and we are all tempted to stop when we reach that point. Yet if we dug further, who knows?—the terrible too might be only a few skins deep" ([1961] 1974, 18–19).

Querry's development, according to the superior's theory, may have been arrested at too early a stage; indeed, Querry may be one of those characters "whose problems arise because they have adopted paradigms of human possibilities which dominate the Western, post-Enlightenment tradition and are found to be inadequate" (Kort 1975, 45). Querry, Greene may well be implying, has discovered the split between what Kierkegaard terms "ideality" and "reality"; the character, depending upon his own power of reason, embraces quite logically a very limited view of human potential because his spiritual development has been cut off; he is like the leper who, as Doctor Colin points out, is free from pain but is subject to "mutilation" as the "alternative" ([1961] 1974, 22). The metaphorical amputation seems quite similar to Kierkegaard's concept of despair of possibility ([1941] 1954, 170–74): Querry's lack of belief evidently causes him to conclude that he has no ethical or religious self which can be actualized. He articulates his despair to Doctor Colin, generalizing upon what he views as the problem of the artist: "Self-expression is a hard and selfish thing. It eats everything, even the self. At the end you find you haven't got a self to express" ([1961] 1974, 46). When Querry unwittingly participates in what Kierkegaard calls the process of repetition, however, he is able to work through his despair and to progress, though haltingly, toward the Kierkegaardian cure of actualized belief.

In *Repetition*, another of the pseudonymous works, Kierkegaard presents two apparently very different characters. One is a young man who, like the historical author himself, has involved a girl in a passionate courtship which he now has no wish to consummate in marriage.[13] The unnamed man experiences guilt because he realizes that, though he has caused the girl to invest her emotions in the relationship, he has never truly loved her and has merely used her as an object of his poetic interest. Confused and severely distressed with self and world, and perhaps considering his indeterminate state a kind of punishment for his actions, he articulates a negative paradigm of himself that demonstrates a lack of belief in human possibility and that is strikingly similar to Querry's emotional/spiritual symptoms of leprosy.

> I am at the end of my rope. I am nauseated by life; it is insipid—without salt and meaning. . . . I stick my finger into the world—it has no smell. Where am I? . . . Who am I . . . How did I get involved in this big enterprise called actuality? Why should I be involved? . . . Guilt—what does it mean? . . . My mind is numb. . . . My whole being screams in self-contradiction. How did it happen that I became guilty? Or am I not guilty? . . . What kind of miserable invention is this human language, which says one thing and means another? (1983b, 200)

But when the young man reads the biblical story of Job's ordeals, he begins to adopt the same point of view as Job, to whom "every human interpretation is only a misconception, and to [whom] in relation to God all his troubles are but a sophism that he, to be sure, cannot solve, but he trusts that God can do it" (1983b, 207). The young man concludes that Job's ordeals were not a punishment and that Job was "in the right" because he admitted being "in the wrong *before God*" (p. 212). In spiritual terms, Job admits his participation in what Kierkegaard considers universal guilt, and he begins his life anew with this knowledge. Job apparently experiences, then, the Kierkegaardian repetition process; it occurred for Job when "every *thinkable* human certainty and probability were impossible"

(p. 212). A synonym for "repetition," Hong and Hong point out in their historical introduction to the book, would be "spontaneity after reflection" or "faith" (pp. xviii–xix). The concept also includes what Alastair Hannay calls a "dependency upon a transcendental origin (and source of value)" (1982, 67).

Repetition, then, is the reliving of one's life from the perspective of faith; it is the existential application of the abstract concept of belief. Job, however, is not truly "a hero of faith," the young man points out, but "disputes at the boundaries of faith are fought out in him" (Kierkegaard 1983b, 210). As a character, then, Job represents someone who can discover his own positive paradigm despite a situation of disjunction and, while doing so, begin to undertake an ethical/spiritual mode of existence. The young man, Kierkegaard suggests, may be able to initiate a similar process in his own life.

The other character in *Repetition* is the pseudonymous author or narrator, Constantin Constantius. Like the historical Kierkegaard, the narrator appears to be a distant, ironic, seemingly objective commentator on the young man's affairs, someone who has "trained [himself] every day for years to have only an objective theoretical interest in people" (1983b, 180). Much like Querry, Constantin offers well-thought-out plans to solve problems; he follows, in other words, a very rationalistic approach to life. Yet, the young man is actually restored to wholeness not by means of Constantin's ideas (which the former rejects as being too "cold and logical as if the world were dead" [p. 191]) but at least partially by an accidental occurrence—the girl's marriage to another man. This fortunate event, together with his understanding of Job's participation in the universal guilt, enables the young man to experience the repetition which bestowed "actuality" (p. 133) upon his existence, almost in spite of the narrator's exclusively cognitive assertions.

Interestingly, though, in the "concluding letter" Constantius reveals that the young man is a fictional character whom he himself has "brought into being" (1983b, 228); Kierkegaard may thus be suggesting that, while reflection and emphasis on impersonal thought processes represent one portion of the narrator's self, this passionate young man is an image of the other part, "the exception" (p. 227) to cognitive understanding. In addition, the narrator describes himself as a "vanishing person" (p. 230) who disappears after delivering the young man unto himself. Both components, then, are assimilated into one person. Reflection and logical thought processes, therefore, seem necessary in the Kierkegaardian schema, but ultimately "spontaneity after reflection," or "repetition" of life experience with a new "God-relationship," can achieve actualization of a positive, or integrated, human self.

Viewing Querry's numbness in the light of *Repetition*, readers can infer that his negative model of himself evidently rests (as the superior suggests) on an assumption, reached at a still superficial level of consciousness, that it is impossible to achieve an integration of ideality and reality, of possibility and necessity. Like Job and the young man, Querry has become aware of his guilt and has determined that the disjunction cannot be dissolved through the use of his reason. But unlike Kierkegaard's characters, Greene's "hero," in the beginning of the journey at least, has not yet accepted this human limitation, for Querry (like Brown in *The Comedians*) is at this point unable to laugh, an action which traditionally suggests a tolerance for human weakness. What may be termed pride in human rationality, therefore, seems to prevent him from "going farther"—Greene uses the metaphor of penetration to indicate that Querry's ethical/spiritual progress is stalled. Yet, despite his negative self-image, while living at the leproserie he does perform a number of actions which, as several of his coworkers point out, clearly resemble the actualization of positive Christian virtues, even if, as Querry so frequently insists, he undertakes these acts of service without having a rational basis for them.

His rescue of his boy, Deo Gratias, from the forest provides one instance of such an act. Perhaps originally prompted by curiosity, Querry plunges more and more deeply into the forest to find the leper and then stays with the frightened boy until daybreak. The act, intentionally neither Christian nor virtuous, nevertheless saves the boy from death. Performing this act, Querry abandons his usual habit of careful reasoning; he becomes, that is, less like the coldly logical Constantin and more like the passionate young man. "He thought: I have no reason to believe that my battery will see me home. He continued to digest the thought as he walked further in. He had said to Doctor Colin to explain the reason for his stay, 'the boat goes no farther,' but it is always possible to go a little deeper on one's own feet" ([1961] 1974, 58–59). Notably, the value Querry attaches to penetration indicates that he views the movement as a positive one—the first sign in the novel of a change in his negative view of himself. He senses the importance of this change as he tells Doctor Colin, "In a way you know this seemed a night when things begin" (p. 61).

The journey does not end even at the next level of awareness, which Querry's dream indicates still later in the story. During his dream Querry finds himself back on the bishop's boat; the metaphor of penetration is repeated to an even stronger degree as Querry describes the boat moving "down the narrowing river into the denser forest. . . . It surprised him to think that he had been so misled as to believe that the boat had reached the furthest point of its journey into the interior when it reached the leproserie. Now he was in motion again, going deeper" ([1961] 1974, 151). Since Querry's original presence on the boat had been a spontaneous act without a logical plan, his return to the boat in the dream confirms the intuitive and emotional aspect of his character.

Another nonrational action that helps break the reader's image of a system of negative traits and also implies an attempt to actualize ideality is Querry's sudden agreement to drive Marie Rycker to Luc, without her husband's knowledge, to determine whether or not she is pregnant. During the trip he considers her needs, however reluctantly. On one occasion, thinking she is crying, he enters her room to comfort her; later, he stops at the church to warn her that her husband has come to Luc angrily seeking her. Thus, his exclusive dependence upon planning and rationality diminishes, just as does Constantin's insistence on his logical planning in *Repetition*. Querry has begun to trust another part of himself; to do so he makes an exception to his enthronement of human cognition.

Perhaps his furthest progression toward actualization of a positive ethical/spiritual self is evident in his ability to laugh at himself, which, however, ironically results in his death from Rycker's gunshots. But at the moment of death, a goal finally appears in the "hero's" muddled quest. For while Querry's interest in and services to the lepers, to Doctor Colin, and to Marie suggest one component of the concept of repetition—the reliving of one's life from a more worthy perspective—Querry's last, unfinished statement seems about to confront what is for Kierkegaard the most crucial ingredient of the process—the relationship with God: "This is absurd or else . . ." ([1961] 1974, 233). After his long history of apparent disbelief, Querry, critically wounded, seems to grasp at the Kierkegaardian alternative. One must choose, evidently, either the absurdity associated with a rational but aesthetic existence, with all its implications of devastating self-disjunction, or its alternative—an ethical/spiritual actuality which also assumes an absurdity: a relationship with God, an acceptance of human limitation, and even a view of suffering as a positive value.[14]

In spite of the pervasive negativity, then, Querry at least envisions the possibility of a positive view of himself and, by extension, of any human being. He has approached the repetition process from the outside in, but in opposition to the falsely pious Rycker and the equally hypocritical journalist, Parkinson, both of whom will remain frozen into the division between ideal and real, Querry reaches the brink of integral selfhood by moving, against human reason, toward the infinite uncertainty—by considering belief instead of the certainty of objective knowledge.

Greene's method of characterization in *A Burnt-Out Case*, then, is to demonstrate emphatically the possibility of a shifting paradigm: he assumes that negative traits and consequent despair can be changed into positive virtue and an ethical/spiritual self, partially through reflection, but mainly through spontaneous human involvement. From a fictional perspective, Greene diverges again from the purely or at least more conventionally modernistic method of self-discovery through exploration of psychological depth to establish what essentially is a Christian model of self-actualization that includes both depth and transcendence. Woolf's "Mrs. Brown," in the hands of Greene, becomes a figure with a new dimension; this model of character, with its sense of accruement, stands in striking opposition to the technique of reductivism found in the characterization of the postmodernist word-being.

Reproducing the positive process of self-actualization in a character, however, is not without its artistic problems. In *Monsignor Quixote* (1982), the author grapples with the conflicts that arise when a character not only embraces transcendental belief in thought but also becomes aware that one must apply that belief to one's "existence," or actions. Such a character is already in the process of achieving a self made in the Kierkegaardian image: he or she, though frequently encountering touches of despair through the recognition of personal failures, nevertheless manages to maintain belief both in possibility and in necessity and struggles to sustain a relationship with God in spite of the world's disjunction. Monsignor Quixote, of course, is just such a character. But he also manifests a troubling—at least for a believer—side-effect; his ultra-Kierkegaardian, passionate interest in eternal salvation seems foolish if not absurd in a contemporary, nonidealistic, essentially nonbelieving, and overwhelmingly chaotic world.[15] Greene's portrayal of the Smiths as comically absurd characters in *The Comedians* is a secularized instance of the same problem. In the case of the Americans, however, the cynical narrator's grudging admission of their positive traits serves to emphasize their devotion and personal effectiveness, thereby allowing many readers to choose to regard them positively and to accept their apparent absurdity.

But the portrayal of the monsignor is somewhat more complicated, for in this novel Greene's ambiguous attack/defense method (see chapter 3) seems to confuse the reader's judgment of the priest's human worth. Greene appears, on the one hand, deliberately to encourage an impression of irrationality, thereby permitting an apparently negative trait system to dominate the characterization. The christening of both major characters with Cervantean names that seem too outlandish to be credible, the insistent personification of the monsignor's car (which he names "Rocinante," after Don Quixote's horse), the many picaresquely styled farcical adventures of all three "characters" (I include the car), in which the monsignor appears foolish and naive, particularly when he tries to apply himself to the world—the condoms mistaken for balloons, the sexual episodes in "The Maiden's Prayer" that surprise the sheltered priest, the monsignor walking through town without shoes, his purple socks filled with holes that mock the dignity of his title—all of these episodes and others tend to underscore the comic absurdity of the priest by confirming his link with Cervantes' mad Quixote.

Also apparently negative is the monsignor's insistent reliance on his old books of theology, an obvious parallel with Quixote's silly, sentimental, chivalric romances. In both cases, the books signify precisely that adherence to theorizing which Johannes Climacus finally admits he is guilty of in *Concluding Unscientific Postscript*—theorizing which Kierkegaard himself so often attacked in his more direct communications (see, for example, 1967–78, 2:2043). The monsignor's use of the formulaic books acts, then, as a failed imitation of the actualization process required of the true Kierkegaardian self. Thus, the believer's attempt to actualize belief appears not only ludicrous but frequently also unsuccessful in achieving its goals.

Possibly supporting the reader's impression of Monsignor Quixote's negative traits is Sancho's repeated valuing of his own philosophy of life rather than Quixote's. Privileging "knowledge" over the priest's "belief," Sancho insists, "I *know* that Marx and Lenin existed. You only believe [in God]" (Greene 1982, 142). Later, Professor Pilbeam also opposes not just religious belief but imaginative belief as well when he tells Father Leopoldo, "I haven't much time for fiction. Facts are what I like" (p. 207).

In these incidents, the artistic problem for the Christian existentialist writer is crystallized: if the character espousing belief appears foolish or naive to other characters and to the readers, then not only is religious belief devalued but the literary product is also implicated in the devaluation, at least for those readers who perceive that a strong parallel exists between the act of suspended disbelief in the work of art (suggested by Greene's continual use of the word "fiction") and the process of believing in a transcendent being.[16] Like the quixotic character who believes in his romances, the artist, too, assumes belief in imagined beings, while in accepting the work of art, the reader grants a similar act of faith. The quixotic character (the idealistic believer), the artist, and the reader, then, all seem to embrace belief to some degree; hence, readers who condemn the absurd monsignor may negate not only the character but the artist and themselves as well.

On the other hand, as in Cervantes' book, the text is sufficiently ambiguous that a reader's negation of quixotism may represent only one possibility; the erection of a system of negative traits may, in fact, reflect not so much Greene's but rather the reader's own enthronement of rationality. The alternate possibility is that Greene, as some critics believe of Cervantes, is defending his character's faith in an apparent absurdity, even at the expense of reason, by so constructing the text as to allow a reader to infer, simultaneously, a structure of far more positive traits. Certainly, the falsity of Querry's logically thought-out conclusions in *A Burnt-Out Case* would prepare the reader for such a dethronement of reason. But Greene subtly presents other hints of this alternate possibility in the text of *Monsignor Quixote*.

The Holy Ghost motif, mentioned on several occasions in the novel, also points toward the danger of relying on reason alone to find truth. The motif begins with Sancho asking Monsignor Quixote to explain why the Holy Ghost is a necessary addendum to the Father and the Son. Attempting to explain the traditionally inexplicable mystery of the Trinity through a rational approach, Quixote compares the Father and the Son to two full bottles of wine. He represents the Holy Ghost by a half bottle, only to realize later that his carefully conceived simile goes against his own sense of truth, for all three Persons, according to Catholic belief, are equal to one another (1982, 50). Human reason, it seems, is too fallible to discern objective reality in a spiritual mystery.[17]

The allusions to Descartes, paradoxically perhaps, serve the same function of demonstrating the limitation of human reason. While this philosopher is usually identified with the espousal of a rational approach to the determination of "certain" knowledge ("I think; therefore, I am"), in the end, as Greene's third-person narrator points out while sketching the background of Father Leopoldo, Descartes found himself accepting an approximation:

> Leopoldo . . . had attached himself to Descartes without thought of where he might be led. He wanted to question everything, in the manner of Descartes, searching for an absolute truth, and in the end, like Descartes, he had accepted what seemed to him the nearest thing to truth. But it was then that he had taken a greater leap than Descartes—a leap into the silent world of Oscera [the monastery]. (1982, 205)

Later, Father Leopoldo himself interprets Descartes's thought as a movement beyond reason: "I suppose Descartes brought me to the point where he brought himself—to faith" (1982, 207). By the time of this statement in the novel, then, not only has the importance of reason in philosophical/religious matters been de-emphasized by characters other than Quixote, but now the necessity of faith—traditionally the antithesis of reason—has also been advanced. Objective knowledge, these characters imply, is impossible for human beings to achieve through the use of their reason; Kierkegaardian subjective truth, however, may be attained through belief.[18] The implied assertion represents, again indirectly, an attack not on the monsignor's real trait system but rather on the apparent negativity by which many readers will perceive any character who passionately espouses belief inwardly. Kierkegaard calls this espousal "subjectivity."

In *Concluding Unscientific Postscript*, Johannes Climacus offers a highly positive view of subjectivity, asserting succinctly that "subjectivity" is "the truth" (Kierkegaard 1968c, 181).[19] Explaining this notion more fully, he maintains that this statement is an "equivalent expression for faith." Subjective truth, then, is *"an objective uncertainty held fast in an appropriation-process of the most passionate inwardness"*; Climacus further enhances the value of this type of truth by insisting that it is "the highest truth attainable for an *existing* [i.e., finite] individual" (p. 182). In this context of subjectivity, Kierkegaard's narrator discusses the Don Quixote figure. At one point, he seems to be assessing the character negatively, saying that Quixote is "the prototype for a subjective madness" (p. 175). But Climacus qualifies the judgment:

> Such a figure would undoubtedly be laughed at, but it is another question with what right; for the fact that the entire age has become passionless constitutes no justification for its laughter. The ludicrousness of the zealot consisted in the fact that his infinite passion had attached itself to a mistaken object (an approximation-object); the good in him was that he had passion. (P. 36)

Kierkegaard expresses directly the need for this type of passion in 1967–78, 3:3133. For him, the error of the quixotic character is not that he manifested the passion but that he is the "unhappy slave of the letter" (1968c, 35). Any individual who is "passionately and infinitely interested in his eternal happiness" is comical, therefore, only "because the objectivity of the Church theory is incommensurable with his interest" (p. 42). By Kierkegaard's standard, then, Monsignor Quixote is negatively comical only when he tries to manage a problem by relying on the (abstract) theology textbooks. But when the "letter," the "approximation-object," the chivalric romances, the theology textbooks, or any such finite manifestation of rules, external authority, and logical explanations ceases to be the main object of interest (which occurs when the priest realizes the error of depending on textbook formulas) and the Infinite Object (God) is substituted instead, then what had been a purely quixotic figure, though still steeped in subjectivity, becomes no longer negatively comical and instead achieves "the culmination of existence," a "unity of the infinite and the finite" through which the individual becomes "most definitely himself" (p. 176). Kierkegaardian subjectivity, or internalized belief in God, then, is a positive trait, for it allows the realization of integral selfhood.

Viewed as one important step in the actualization process, Monsignor Quixote's "absurd" qualities may, upon closer examination, begin to reveal themselves as part of a trait cluster that is far more positive than first appearances would suggest. In fact, the very use of the term "absurd," appearing frequently in Greene's novel, may imply still another parallel with positive Kierkegaardian thought. Climacus's definition of "absurd" is revealing:

> What now is the absurd? The absurd is—that the eternal truth has come into being in time, that God has come into being, has been born, has grown up, and so forth, precisely like any other individual human being, quite indistinguishable from other individuals. . . . the absurd is the object of faith, and the only object that can be *believed* [rather than *known*]. (Kierkegaard 1968, 188–89; italics mine)

Furthermore, "The absurd . . . involves the contradiction that something which can become historical only in direct opposition to all human reason, has become historical" (p. 189; cf. 1967–78, 2:1642).

Interestingly, Monsignor Quixote and Sancho use "absurd" in a similar context during a conversation in which the former maintains that he has faith in "historic fact. That Christ died on the Cross and rose again." Sancho calls that "fact" the "greatest absurdity of all" (Greene 1982, 77). Thus, the "absurd," or what Kierkegaard calls "the Absolute Paradox" (1936, 29), though it collides with reason and therefore may at first appear negative, may actually function positively as the means through which the individual progresses to faith and therefore, in Kierkegaard's opinion, to an actualized self. In part 2 of Greene's novel, Monsignor Quixote, by performing the Catholic Mass, clearly participates in this ultimate "absurdity."[20] He thereby becomes the quintessence of Kierkegaardian subjectivity, exhibiting a faith that emanates no longer from theological textbooks but from an actualization of his own inwardness, his own belief in unity—a realization, in Kierkegaardian terms, of his true self. Like Querry at the moment of death, Monsignor Quixote, too, experiences Kierkegaard's repetition process; that is, he relives his experience (in his second journey) from the vantage point not of objective church rules but of inward, passionate faith.

At such a moment, again if the reader chooses, the value of the artistic production can also be restored to its former privileged position, for though the rigid, formulaic textbooks may be unsuitable, other books—Quixote's books of saints, specifically, representing acts of love rather than rules—are just as eagerly embraced. But even more important than the product of art, the act of creation itself, the same kind of act by which the individual accepts religious belief and by which the artist and reader suspend imaginative disbelief, can be viewed positively, in the context of Kierkegaardian thought, as a means by which a reader may choose to discover eternal truth. "Fiction," then, as El Saffar has affirmed, "is not devoid of meaning, for it is part of a dialectical process through which transcendent reality is finally achieved" (1974, 27). What had appeared to be a negative trait, or at least what is often regarded as such from an external viewpoint, can also be inherently positive—if the reader makes a different kind of choice.

In the characterization of Monsignor Quixote, then, inwardness can be an eminently valuable asset that bears fruit after a gestation period of dialectical reflection. When individuals allow the relationship with God to devastate their reason (note that Quixote's brain is "fragmented"), they may discover the "heart of the matter" that Scobie (or Brown) never found. Through belief that is existentially applied, Greene indicates, the self is finally actualized. And it makes its mark gently yet lastingly, Sancho finds, through its manifestation of trust and love.

Thus, Greene's multifaceted method of exploring character moves from an *apparent* system of traits to a truer, spiritually-based cluster, yielding the actualized self which Greene assumes is always potentially present. His technique, moreover, crosses the imaginary boundaries among literary eras: for Greene, as for Kierkegaard, "Mrs. Brown" is neither purely a social being nor merely an unconscious one; she is not fashioned only of language or of negation. She is all of these, for the Christian artist, but she is more besides: she has a soul which she may choose to entomb or to enshrine, and because of it, her apparent nothingness is merely a facade.

Greene has effectively and perseveringly created, then, during his fifty-year career, many kinds of spiritualized Mrs. Browns in various stages of negativity and positivity. Teasingly, yet also seriously, he invites each reader to join them in the carriage, to decide dialectically the meaning and value of their apparent traits, and to discover whether these traits remain as abstractions or become concretized in the characters' lives. If readers respond as Kierkegaard and Greene would hope, they will make the connection between literature and life and will identify, however painfully, with each character's unique type of success or, more frequently, failure to actualize the subjective self. With Greene's technique of characterization, therefore, the ideal reader *becomes* Mrs. Brown and faces, as did Monsignor Quixote and Søren Kierkegaard, a potentially shattering and yet unifying choice that is fully as absurd as accepting a character in a book but that produces a much more radical effect on human life. Greene seems to agree, finally, with Kierkegaard's most outrageous assertion: "The judgment . . . that He exists . . . is the decision for the whole of existence" ([1941] 1954, 260).

Conclusion

In the light of the Kierkegaardian canon, Greene's fluctuating irony, his use of dialectical structures, his double-edged method of presenting a character, his view of the self as a potentially integral spiritual "reality," and his insistence on an existential appropriation of abstraction combine to indicate a discourse of belief. Greene's methods are partly traditional but also carry modern and even postmodern overtones, for while Greene upholds the formal structures and the moral emphasis of his past, he remains strikingly current in his implication of the world's apparently permanent state of disjunction. Moreover, his general absence from the text and lack of overt prodding for the reader's response not only remove him from a possibly offensive, evangelical approach to belief but allow him also to confront the reader with the dilemma of choice among many existential possibilities.

The choice is not between absurdity versus meaning, for with Greene, as with Kierkegaard, a Transcendental Absurdity *is* the meaning. The choice, instead, is whether, through passion and will, to achieve a humanity invested with an integral eternity or whether, with passivity and fallible logic, to continue alone in finite futility.

By adding spiritual fervor to abstract imagination, then, Greene attempts to restore the value both of religious belief and of the artistic endeavor. While in his configuration the literary text is not itself a god-figure, it exists at least partially as a means to discover what Greene considers a real and objective God-figure subjectively. Such a view of the text, obviously, is political, but no more and no less so than, for example, many postmodernist endeavors to present the text, the fictional character, and, by implication, the human self as purely linguistic entities. A discourse suggesting transcendental belief, therefore, need not remove a Christian artist from the so-called mainstream of modern and contemporary fiction, for in a society that is at least nominally free, all literature should be accorded equal liberty to state its individual views. In this context, artists will be judged not so much by their difference from other artists but by the degree of success they demonstrate in presenting their own imagination.

Notes

1: Form, Standpoint, and Existential Possibility

1. See also the commentaries by Clancey (1956), O'Brien (1966), Allott and Farris ([1951] 1963), and Kunkel (1973).
2. According to Wilde, mediate irony "imagines a world lapsed from a recoverable . . . norm," while suspensive irony posits a "yet more radical vision of multiplicity, randomness, contingency, and even absurdity." In suspensive irony, "the world in all its disorder is simply (or not so simply) accepted"; "ambiguity and paradox give way to quandary, to a low-keyed engagement with a world of perplexities and uncertainties" (1981, 10).
3. Critics who assert a similar purpose for Kierkegaard's use of irony include Diem (1959, 42) and Nagley (1981, 40).
4. See, for instance, Duncan (1976, 31–54), Diem (1966, 7–17), and Hannay (1982, 19–53).
5. Stack offers a similar opinion: "Kierkegaard believed that the ironic standpoint of Socrates (in its purely negative form) must be transcended" (1977, 3).
6. Though not all "existential possibilities" (potential ways of living) need be presented ironically, of course, those which are rendered negatively (yet not necessarily unsympathetically) become "ironic." Crites interprets Kierkegaard's ironic/aesthetic works as dramatizations of existential possibilities, maintaining that the author presents each "stage" in *Stages on*

Life's Way as "a richly rendered life-possibility" (1972, 201). See also Mackey, who asserts that Kierkegaard's "'intent' is to exfoliate existential possibilities" (1972, 97). I am grateful to Daniel O'Hara for directing me to the approach in these essays.

2: Author, Narrator, and Reader

1. "Object" seems to refer to specific information conveyed to a receiver by the text or discourse itself. For a written communication, "communicator" and "receiver" refer to author and reader respectively; the "communication," defined later in the *Journals* (1:651), is "the medium," or in literary terms, the form of discourse.

2. Diem interprets "dialogue" quite broadly: "Everything which [Kierkegaard] makes his fictitious characters say moves within the sphere of dualistic Socratic dialectic. In truth, he did not renounce the dialogue form, but made one single sustained dialogue of the entire work of his pseudonymous characters. The reader takes the place of the conversational partner" (1959, 41).

3. Johannes is not a professional creative artist in the specific sense of the term except insofar as he is a writer of the diary, but he is an artist figure, or someone who performs his "work" (seduction) as if it were an art.

4. See *Sickness unto Death* ([1941] 1954) for Kierkegaard's definition and analysis of several kinds of despair, a theme which I discuss in chapter 4.

5. Johan Ludvig Heiberg (1791–1860) was a Danish dramatist and reviewer who had criticized *Either/Or* rather harshly at first, finding the earlier volume "offensive and disgusting," as Lowrie explains in the translator's introduction to the second volume (1971, 2:xvii).

6. The narrator of the diary is actually not named; "quidam" refers to an unspecified person. The story recounted in the diary, however, is thought to resemble strongly Kierkegaard's actual engagement with Regina Olsen, which he felt compelled to break because of his religious inclinations. The ending of the relationship, according to Lowrie, caused both a great deal of grief ([1941] 1951, 131–43).

7. In her book-length interview with Greene, Marie-Françoise Allain calls him in a chapter heading "The Secret Man," noting that Greene "tends to see himself as one of his characters" (1983, 15).

8. Martin Turnell, for example, confuses the two views by asserting that occurrences in the novel such as Pinkie's brooding over "the frightening weekly exercise of his parents" or the use of diction referring to the sex act as "dirty scramble" "reveal a view of human nature that is warped to the point of abnormality" (1961, 63). Since in criticism the author is conventionally expected to exhibit a "view of human nature," one can infer that Turnell is objecting to what he assumes is Greene's view, not Pinkie's.

9. See Gransden 1981, which includes an analysis of Greene's use of the simile in his early novels and entertainments.

3: The Force of Ambiguity

1. Hans Martensen succeeded Mynster as bishop of Zealand.

2. In addition to Lowrie, Elmer H. Duncan, as well as several other critics, finds that the "attack was mounted from *within* the church" (1976, 25).

3. Alastair Hannay affirms the same interpretation in his chapter on Kierkegaard's politics by noting that, when a group assumes primacy, "the *idea* of a collectivity" is "spuriously given the status of a *thing*" (1982, 283). The false assumption, Hannay contends, is that "properly *human* action is necessarily collective action" (p. 285). In *Training in Christianity*, Kierkegaard attacks this limiting of the individual to his or her membership in the established church, not the establishment itself.

4: Toward an Actual Self

1. Cf. George Eliot's mention of "the persistent self" in chapter 15 of *Middlemarch*.

2. These patterns may also be negatively presented, however; for example, in *The Mill on the Floss*, Eliot seems to perceive Maggie's feminine self-development as an ambivalent and dangerous, though necessary, force.

3. I thank Alan Wilde for bringing Weinstein's analysis to my attention.

4. These representations are my own; Kierkegaard does not, to my knowledge, use graphic illustrations to describe the self.

5. Robert Langbaum (1977) notes the literary use of the death-in-life experience in what he calls the theme of "the walking dead" (though he

does not connect it with Kierkegaard); Ford's *Good Soldier* and Eliot's *Waste Land*, Langbaum states, convey the same theme in early twentieth-century literature.

6. More than one narrator may well be speaking in the "Diapsalmata," since the work contains a series of different aphoristic commentaries on a variety of subjects. Because the number of narrators would be difficult if not impossible to prove, however, I will, for the sake of discussion, treat the speeches as though spoken by a single voice.

7. *Brighton Rock* and *The Power and the Glory* are two other early treatments of self-killing.

8. Although events are recounted by a grammatical third-person narrator, most of the novel presents Scobie's own viewpoint, with only an occasional comment by the implied author.

9. "It is only responsibility that bestows a blessing and true joy" (Kierkegaard 1971, 2:87).

10. Maurice Crubellier (1951) and Conor Cruise O'Brien ([1952] 1963) also comment on Greene's negative use of pity.

11. Kierkegaard defines these two terms as follows: "The self . . . is just as possible as it is necessary; for though it is itself, it has to become itself. Inasmuch as it is itself, it is the necessary, and inasmuch as it has to become itself, it is a possibility" ([1941] 1954, 168).

12. Van Kaam and Healy regard Querry's characterization similarly, stating that his "self-revulsion" is also his own "hidden self-divinization" (1967, 61).

13. *Repetition* is another of Kierkegaard's fictional renderings of his own relationship with Regina Olsen; the framework of the plot closely resembles the situation in "Quidam's Diary" in *Stages on Life's Way*.

14. See Kierkegaard's *Philosophical Fragments* for his discussion of what he considers equally absurd—the union of the finite and the infinite in the birth of Christ.

15. See also Flannery O'Connor's similar comments on the modern reader's attitude to this kind of character (1969, 42).

16. I owe my perception of this parallel at least in part to Marthe Robert's fine book-length study (1977) of the quixotic novel as rendered by Cervantes and by Kafka; see especially pp. 42–57.

17. To draw such an inference from the novel, however, is not to assert that Greene denies objective reality. I believe his dethronement of pure reason suggests only, as El Saffar points out in her critique of Cervantes'

works, that "perceived reality, when measured against transcendent reality, is as a fiction" (1974, 27).

18. "Subjective" truth for Kierkegaard does not mean "relative" truth; nor should the term, as he uses it, be confused with the modernists' use of the word "subjectivism," which generally refers to a purely psychological process of internalization that lacks any spiritual component and results not in the formulation but rather in the disintegration of the self.

19. While Johannes Climacus (pseudonym) has views that cannot necessarily be trusted, his statements quoted here clearly reflect Kierkegaard's own opinion, since, to begin with, several passages in the *Journals* also cite the crucial importance of "subjectivity" (see, for example, 4:4555, 4564). I use Climacus's phraseology because it offers a more compact yet precise explanation of the concept than does any one passage in the *Journals*. In addition, though, Kierkegaard himself, in *Point of View*, notes an important difference between *Concluding Unscientific Postscript* and the other pseudonymous works: "The *Concluding Postscript* is not an aesthetic work, but neither is it in the strictest sense religious. Hence it is by a pseudonym, though I add my name as editor—a thing I did not do in the case of any purely aesthetic work" (1962a, 13). Perhaps Kierkegaard is willing to add his own name, since not only the passages on subjectivity but other ideas in *Concluding Unscientific Postscript* are also duplicated in his direct writings. Hence, the work may be ironic, not because all Climacus's reflections are, for Kierkegaard, invalid (clearly, many are not), but because they remain, for Climacus, *only* reflections; he admits that he does not actualize them in his own existence. He himself is not a true Christian; thus, he retracts his own book. Other critics who point out or assume similarities between Kierkegaard's ideas and the ideas of a pseudonym include Josiah Thompson (1967, 197–99) and Gregor Malantschuk (1971, 307). Gill, however, rightly cautions against the danger of too facile a linkage between Kierkegaard and his pseudonyms (1981, 205).

20. Even more absurd is Quixote's saying the Mass without chalice or host but acting as if these substances are present in his hands.

Works Cited

Allain, Marie-Françoise. 1983. *The Other Man: Conversations with Graham Greene*. Trans. Guido Waldman. New York: Simon and Schuster.

Allott, Kenneth, and Miriam Farris. [1951] 1963. *The Art of Graham Greene*. Reprint. New York: Russell and Russell.

Anderson, Raymond Eugene. 1966. *Kierkegaard's Theory of Communication*. Ann Arbor: University Microfilms.

Barratt, Harold. 1965. "Adultery as Betrayal in Graham Greene." *Dalhousie Review* 45:324–32.

Barthes, Roland. [1953] 1967. Introduction to *Writing Degree Zero*, trans. Annette Lavers and Colin Smith, 1–6. Reprint. New York: Hill and Wang.

Booth, Wayne C. 1961. *The Rhetoric of Fiction*. Chicago: University of Chicago Press.

Brown, Marshall. 1984. "'Errours Endlesse Traine': On Turning Points and the Dialectical Imagination." *PMLA* 99:9–25.

Burgess, Anthony. 1967. "Politics in the Novels of Graham Greene." *Journal of Contemporary History* 2:92–99.

———. 1982. "A Talk with Graham Greene." *Saturday Review*, May, 44–47.

Cervantes Saavedra, Miguel de. 1977. *Don Quixote of La Mancha*. Trans. Walter Starkie. New York: New American Library.

Works Cited

Chatman, Seymour. 1978. *Story and Discourse: Narrative Structure in Fiction and Film.* Ithaca: Cornell University Press.

Cirlot, J. E. 1962. *A Dictionary of Symbols.* Trans. Jack Sage. New York: Philosophical Library.

Clancey, William. 1956. "The Moral Burden of Mr. Greene's Parable." *Commonweal* 63:622.

Coleman, Patrick. 1983. "Character in an Eighteenth-Century Context." *Eighteenth Century: Theory and Interpretation* 24:51–63.

Conrad, Joseph. [1910] 1950. *Heart of Darkness and the Secret Sharer.* Reprint. New York: New American Library.

Crites, Stephen. 1972. "Pseudonymous Authorship as Art and as Act." In *Kierkegaard: A Collection of Critical Essays,* ed. Josiah Thompson, 183–229. Garden City, N.Y.: Doubleday Anchor.

Crubellier, Maurice. 1951. "Graham Greene: La tragédie de la pitié." *Vie intellectuelle* 12:57–78.

Diem, Hermann. 1959. *Kierkegaard's Dialectic of Existence.* Trans. Harold Knight. Edinburgh: Oliver and Boyd.

———. 1966. *Kierkegaard: An Introduction.* Richmond: John Knox Press.

Dillistone, F. W. 1955. *Christianity and Symbolism.* London: Collins.

Duncan, Elmer H. 1976. *Søren Kierkegaard.* Waco, Tex.: Word Books.

El Saffar, Ruth S. 1974. *Novel to Romance: A Study of Cervantes's "Novelas ejemplares."* Baltimore: Johns Hopkins University Press.

Evans, Robert O. 1957. "Existentialism in Greene's *The Quiet American.*" *Modern Fiction Studies* 3:241–48.

Federman, Raymond. 1981a. "Fiction Today or the Pursuit of Non-Knowledge." In *Surfiction: Fiction Now . . . and Tomorrow.* 2d ed., ed. Raymond Federman, 291–311. Chicago: Swallow Press.

———. 1981b. "Surfiction—Four Propositions in Form of an Introduction." In *Surfiction: Fiction Now . . . and Tomorrow.* 2d ed., ed. Raymond Federman, 5–15. Chicago: Swallow Press.

Fish, Stanley. 1980. "Interpreting the Variorum." In *Reader-Response Criticism: From Formalism to Post-Structuralism,* ed. Jane P. Tompkins, 164–84. Baltimore: Johns Hopkins University Press.

Ford, Ford Madox. [1927] 1951. *The Good Soldier.* Reprint. New York: Random House.

Genette, Gérard. 1980. *Narrative Discourse: An Essay in Method.* Trans. Jane E. Lewin. Ithaca: Cornell University Press.

Gill, Jerry H. 1981. "Faith Is As Faith Does." In *Kierkegaard's "Fear and Trembling": Critical Appraisals*, ed. Robert L. Perkins, 204–17. University: University of Alabama Press.

Gransden, K. W. 1981. "Graham Greene's Rhetoric." *Essays in Criticism* 31:41–60.

Greene, Graham. [1938] 1970. *Brighton Rock.* Reprint. London: W. Heinemann and Bodley Head.

———. [1940] 1971. *The Power and the Glory.* Reprint. London: W. Heinemann and Bodley Head.

———. [1948] 1971. *The Heart of the Matter.* Reprint. London: W. Heinemann and Bodley Head.

———. [1951] 1974. *The End of the Affair.* Reprint. London: W. Heinemann and Bodley Head.

———. [1955] 1973. *The Quiet American.* Reprint. London: W. Heinemann and Bodley Head.

———. [1961] 1974. *A Burnt-Out Case.* Reprint. London: W. Heinemann and Bodley Head.

———. 1962. *In Search of a Character.* New York: Viking Press.

———. [1966] 1976. *The Comedians.* Reprint. London: W. Heinemann and Bodley Head.

———. 1969. *Collected Essays.* London: Bodley Head.

———. 1971. *A Sort of Life.* New York: Simon and Schuster.

———. [1972] 1981. *Travels with My Aunt.* Reprint. New York: Viking Press.

———. [1973] 1980. *The Honorary Consul.* Reprint. London: W. Heinemann and Bodley Head.

———. 1978. *The Human Factor.* New York: Simon and Schuster.

———. [1980a] 1981. *Doctor Fischer of Geneva or the Bomb Party.* Reprint. New York: Avon Books.

———. 1980b. *Ways of Escape.* New York: Simon and Schuster.

———. 1982. *Monsignor Quixote.* New York: Simon and Schuster.

Hanlon, Robert M. 1977. "The Ascent to Belief in Graham Greene's *A Burnt-Out Case.*" *Christianity and Literature* 26:20–26.

Hannay, Alastair. 1982. *Kierkegaard.* London: Routledge and Kegan Paul.

Harvey, W. J. 1965. *Character and the Novel.* London: Chatto and Windus.

Hochman, Baruch. 1983. *The Test of Character: From the Victorian Novel to the Modern.* Rutherford, N.J.: Fairleigh Dickinson University Press.

Iser, Wolfgang. 1978. *The Act of Reading: A Theory of Aesthetic Response.* Baltimore: Johns Hopkins University Press.

James, Henry. [1900] 1974. "The Great Good Place." *American Literature: Tradition and Innovation,* ed. Harrison T. Meserole, Walter Sutton, and Brom Weber, 2546–66. Reprint. Lexington, Mass.: Heath.

———. 1908. Preface to *The Awkward Age,* v-xxiv. New York: Scribner's.

Kern, Edith. 1970. *Existential Thought and Fictional technique: Kierkegaard, Sartre, Beckett.* New Haven: Yale University Press.

Kierkegaard, Søren. 1936. *Philosophical Fragments or a Fragment of Philosophy.* Trans. David S. Swenson. Princeton: Princeton University Press.

———. 1940. *Stages on Life's Way.* Trans. Walter Lowrie. Princeton: Princeton University Press.

———. [1941] 1954. "The Sickness unto Death." In *Fear and Trembling* and *The Sickness unto Death,* trans. Walter Lowrie, 133–262. Reprint. Garden City, N.Y.: Doubleday.

———. [1944a] 1968. *Kierkegaard's Attack upon "Christendom."* Trans. Walter Lowrie. Reprint. Princeton: Princeton University Press.

———. 1944b. *Training in Christianity.* Trans. Walter Lowrie. Princeton: Princeton University Press.

———. 1962a. *The Point of View for My Work as an Author.* Trans. Walter Lowrie, ed. Benjamin Nelson. New York: Harper and Brothers.

———. 1962b. *Works of Love: Some Christian Reflections in the Form of Discourses.* Trans. Howard Hong and Edna Hong. New York: Harper and Row.

———. 1967–78. *Søren Kierkegaard's Journals and Papers.* 7 vols. Ed. and trans. Howard V. Hong and Edna H. Hong, assisted by Gregor Malantschuk. Bloomington: Indiana University Press.

———. 1968a. *Armed Neutrality.* Ed. and trans. Howard V. Hong and Edna H. Hong. New York: Simon and Schuster.

———. 1968b. *The Concept of Irony.* Trans. Lee M. Capel. Bloomington: Indiana University Press.

———. 1968c. *Kierkegaard's "Concluding Unscientific Postscript."* Trans. David F. Swenson and Walter Lowrie. Princeton: Princeton University Press.

———. 1971. *Either/Or.* 2 vols. Trans. (vol. 1) David F. Swenson and

Lillian Marvin Swenson, (vol. 2) Walter Lowrie; rev. Howard A. Johnson. Princeton: Princeton University Press.

———. 1983a. "Fear and Trembling." In *Fear and Trembling* and *Repetition*, ed. and trans. Howard V. Hong and Edna H. Hong, 5–123. Princeton: Princeton University Press.

———. 1983b. "Repetition." In *Fear and Trembling* and *Repetition*, ed. and trans. Howard V. Hong and Edna H. Hong, 125–231. Princeton: Princeton University Press.

Kort, Wesley A. 1975. *Narrative Elements and Religious Meaning*. Philadelphia: Fortress Press.

Kunkel, Francis L. 1973. *The Labyrinthine Ways of Graham Greene*. 2d. ed. Mamaroneck, N.Y.: Appel.

Langbaum, Robert. 1977. *The Mysteries of Identity: A Theme in Modern Literature*. New York: Oxford University Press.

Lanser, Susan Sniader. 1981. *The Narrative Act: Point of View in Prose Fiction*. Princeton: Princeton University Press.

Larsen, Eric. 1976. "Reconsideration: *The Quiet American*." *New Republic* 175:40–42.

Laurence, Margaret. 1978. "Ivory Tower or Grassroots? The Novelist as Socio-Political Being." In *A Political Art: Essays and Images in Honour of George Woodcock*, ed. William H. New, 15–25. Vancouver: University of British Columbia Press.

Lerner, Laurence. 1964. "Love and Gossip; or, How Moral Is Literature?" *Essays in Criticism* 14:126–47.

Letwin, Shirley Robin. 1983. "Finished and Unfinished Selves." Review of *The Test of Character: From the Victorian Novel to the Modern*, by Baruch Hochman. *Times Literary Supplement*, 30 December, 1447–48.

Levin, Gerald. 1970. "The Rhetoric of Greene's *The Heart of the Matter*." *Renascence* 23:14–20.

Lowrie, Walter. [1941] 1951. *A Short Life of Kierkegaard*. Reprint. Princeton: Princeton University Press.

Mackey, Louis. 1969. "Kierkegaard and the Problem of Existential Philosophy." In *Essays on Kierkegaard*, ed. Jerry H. Gill, 31–57. Minneapolis: Burgess.

———. 1972. "The Poetry of Inwardness." In *Kierkegaard: A Collection of Critical Essays*, ed. Josiah Thompson, 1–102. Garden City, N.Y.: Doubleday Anchor.

Malantschuk, Gregor. 1971. *Kierkegaard's Thought.* Ed. and trans. Howard V. Hong and Edna H. Hong. Princeton: Princeton University Press.

Marian, Sister. 1965. "Graham Greene's People: Being and Becoming." *Renascence* 18:16–22.

Meixner, John A. 1962. *Ford Madox Ford's Novels: A Critical Study.* Minneapolis: University of Minnesota Press.

Nagley, Winifred. 1981. "Irony in the 'Diapsalmata.'" In *Kierkegaard: Literary Miscellany,* ed. Neils Thulstrup and M. Mikulova Thulstrup, 24–54. Copenhagen: C. A. Reitzels Boghandel.

Noxon, James. 1962. "Kierkegaard's Stages and *A Burnt-Out Case.*" *Review of English Literature* 3:90–101.

O'Brien, Conor Cruise. [1952] 1963. "Graham Greene: The Anatomy of Pity." Chapter 3 in *Maria Cross: Imaginative Patterns in A Group of Catholic Writers,* 57–83. Reprint. London: Burns and Oates.

———. 1966. "Old Black Magic Has Him in Its Spell." *Book Week* 3 (6 February): 5.

O'Connor, Flannery. 1969. *Mystery and Manners.* Ed. Sally Fitzgerald and Robert Fitzgerald. New York: Farrar, Straus, and Giroux.

Pascal, Roy. 1977. *The Dual Voice: Free Indirect Speech and Its Functioning in the Nineteenth-Century European Novel.* Manchester: Manchester University Press.

Robert, Marthe. 1977. *The Old and the New: From "Don Quixote" to Kafka.* Trans. Carol Cosman. Berkeley: University of California Press.

Ruotolo, Lucio P. 1964. "*Brighton Rock*'s Absurd Heroine." *Modern Language Quarterly* 25:425–33.

Schmidt, S. J. 1975. "Reception and Interpretation of Written Texts as Problems of a Rational Theory of Literary Communication." In *Style and Text: Studies Presented to Nils Erik Enkvist.* Ed. H'akan Ringbom et al. 399–408. Stockholm: Sprakforlaget Skriptor.

Scott, Nathan A., Jr. 1956. "Catholic Novelist's Dilemma." *Christian Century* 73:901–2.

Spender, Stephen. 1978. "Poetry." In *The Writer and Politics,* vol. 11 of *Literary Taste, Culture, and Mass Communication,* ed. Peter Davison, Rolf Meyersohn, and Edward Shils, 128–40. Cambridge: Chadwyck-Healey; Teaneck, N.J.: Somerset House.

Stack, George J. 1977. *Kierkegaard's Existential Ethics.* University: University of Alabama Press.

Works Cited

Taylor, Mark C. 1975. *Kierkegaard's Pseudonymous Authorship.* Princeton: Princeton University Press.

Thompson, Josiah. 1967. *The Lonely Labyrinth: Kierkegaard's Pseudonymous Works.* Carbondale: Southern Illinois University Press.

———. 1972. "The Mastery of Irony." In *Kierkegaard: A Collection of Critical Essays,* ed. Josiah Thompson, 103–63. Garden City, N.Y.: Doubleday Anchor.

Tompkins, Jane P. 1980. "An Introduction to Reader-Response Criticism." In *Reader-Response Criticism: From Formalism to Post-Structuralism,* ed. Jane P. Tompkins, ix–xxvi. Baltimore: Johns Hopkins University Press.

Trilling, Diana, and Philip Rahv. 1956. "America and *The Quiet American.*" *Commentary* 22:66–71.

Turnell, Martin. 1961. *Modern Literature and Christian Faith.* London: Darton, Langman and Todd.

———. 1967. *Graham Greene: A Critical Essay.* Grand Rapids, Mich.: Eerdmans.

Van Kaam, Adrian, and Kathleen Healy. 1967. *The Demon and the Dove: Personality Growth through Literature.* Pittsburgh: Duquesne University Press.

Webster, Harvey Curtis. 1963. "The World of Graham Greene." In *Graham Greene: Some Critical Considerations,* ed. Robert O. Evans, 1–24. Lexington: University of Kentucky Press.

Weinstein, Arnold. 1981. *Fictions of the Self, 1550–1800.* Princeton: Princeton University Press.

Weselinski, Andrzej. 1976. "Irony and Melodrama in *The Heart of the Matter.*" *Studia Anglica Posnaniensia* 8:167–73.

White, George Abbott, and Charles Newman, eds. 1972. *Literature in Revolution.* New York: Holt, Rinehart and Winston.

Wilde, Alan. 1981. *Horizons of Assent: Modernism, Postmodernism, and the Ironic Imagination.* Baltimore: Johns Hopkins University Press.

Woolf, Virginia. [1924] 1950. "Mr. Bennett and Mrs. Brown." In *The Captain's Death Bed and Other Essays,* 90–111. Reprint. London: Hogarth Press.

Index

Aesthetic, 21, 22, 24–25, 30–31, 33, 35, 38–40, 42, 77–78, 97, 112 (n. 19)
Ambiguity, 44–45, 51, 53–54, 59
Art, 23, 38–40; art novel, 1–2; of writing, 35
Artist, 35–36, 92
Attack-defense method, 46, 48–56, 59–60, 62–64, 98
Attack upon "Christendom," 47–48, 51, 58, 65–66

Belief, 11–12, 16, 40–43, 51–52, 71, 74, 76, 78, 82–83, 85, 87–88, 91–93, 97–100, 103–104, 106
Bildungsroman, 68
Brighton Rock, xvi, 3, 28–29, 31–35, 111 (n. 7)
Burnt-Out Case, A, 3, 13, 16, 29, 64, 90–98, 100

Capability, 18, 20, 27, 29, 39–40, 42, 46, 48, 51, 59
Comedians, The, 3, 4, 43, 82–90, 95
Communication, 18, 35;
 direct: 29, 46; defined, 18;
 indirect: 21, 24–25, 27–29, 31, 34, 40, 43, 45, 48, 59, 72; defined, 18
Concept of Irony, The, 6, 9–12
Concluding Unscientific Postscript, 17, 42, 46, 51, 55, 62, 72, 99, 101, 112 (n. 19)
Conrad, Joseph, 1, 2, 13

Despair, 43, 72, 74, 80, 86, 89, 91–92, 97–98, 109 (n. 4)
Dialectical formation, 21, 24, 31, 34–35, 45. *See also* Oppositional perspective
Discourse, 106–107, 109 (n. 1); defined, xv
Disguise, 19, 30. *See also* Incognito

Either/Or, 21, 26, 33–35, 38, 41–42, 72, 74–75, 77, 109 (n. 5)
End of the Affair, The, 15, 29, 35–43
Ethical, 21, 24–26, 78, 94, 97. *See also* Capability
Existence, 11, 98
Existential, 11, 13–14, 16, 21, 24–26, 33, 35, 42, 47, 56, 61–63, 66, 71, 75–76, 82, 90, 99, 104, 106, 108–109 (n. 6)

120

Index

Father, 60–61, 63–65; fatherhood, 62
Fear and Trembling, 64
Ford, Ford Madox, 1, 2, 13
Form, 5, 12; traditional novel, 5, 13, 16
Free indirect style, 31–33, 64, 78

Gun for Sale, A, xvi

Heart of the Matter, The, 4, 14–15, 28–29, 33, 76–81
Hegel, 9
Heiberg, Johan Ludvig, 12, 23, 109 (n. 5)
Honorary Consul, The, 29, 31, 60–66
Human Factor, The, xvi

Incognito: artistic, 27. *See also* Disguise
Individual, 49–51, 59–60, 63, 65–66, 72, 75, 102, 104
Infinite absolute negativity, 7, 9, 13. *See also* Standpoint, negative
Irony, xiii, 6–7, 12, 19, 40; disjunctive, 5, 7, 12, 16, 49, 60, 63, 88–89, 91, 94–95, 98, 106; mediate, 5, 108 (n. 2); suspensive, 5, 108 (n. 2); mastered, 7–9, 11
Iser, Wolfgang, 20

James, Henry, 1–3, 13, 29–30, 32, 87–88
Journals, 6, 10, 46, 99, 112 (n. 19)

Modernism, 12, 69, 71, 75, 81, 89–91, 97, 107
Monsignor Quixote, 3, 16, 29, 98–105

Oppositional perspective, 21, 23–24, 40–41, 43; in text, 26. *See also* Dialectical formation

Philosphical Fragments, 111 (n. 14)
Point of View for My Work As an Author, The, 10, 18, 21, 30, 112 (n. 19)
Political: defined, 45; realities, 52; motives, 53; situation, 60, 61; condition, 63; solution, 66

Politics, 44, 48, 54
Postmodern, 71, 75, 81–82, 89–90, 98, 106–107
Power and the Glory, The, xvi, 3, 15, 29, 31, 33, 64, 111 (n. 7)
Pseudonym, 42
Pseudonymous, 19; works, 6, 21, 93, 112 (n. 19); author, 24, 72, 94; characters, 109 (n. 2)

Quiet American, The, xvi, 3, 4, 14, 51–60

Reader-response, 20, 27, 32, 48, 52–54, 60, 100, 104–106
Religious way of life, 24–26
Repetition, 71, 93–96, 111 (n. 13)

Self, 9, 16, 27, 42, 67–72, 74–75, 78, 80–82, 84, 86–87, 89–90, 93, 95, 97–99, 103–107, 110 (n. 1, n. 4), 111 (n. 11), 112 (n. 18)
Selfhood, 73, 76, 83
Sickness Unto Death, 71–72, 74, 80, 86
Socrates, 6, 7, 19, 108 (n. 5)
Sort of Life, A, 2, 5
Stages on Life's Way, 25, 75, 111 (n. 13)
Standpoint, 4–8, 11–13, 16–17, 84, 91, 108 (n. 5); negative, 6, 12–13, 27, 39, 66, 75–76, 86, 88–91, 93, 95–97 (*see also* Infinite absolute negativity); mobile, 8–9, 13, 17, 40, 48, 75
Subjective: Christianity, 46; existence, 48; truth, 112 (n. 18)
Subjectivity, 20, 29, 101–103, 112 (n. 19)

Training in Christianity, 45, 49, 50–51, 110 (n. 3)
Travels With My Aunt, 3, 4, 16, 43
Truth, 10, 16, 31, 101–102

Ways of Escape, 4, 28, 30
Woolf, Virginia, 67–71, 90, 98
Works of Love, 65

121

About the Author

Anne T. Salvatore teaches English at Rider College. She received her doctorate from Temple University, her master's degree from Trenton State College, and her bachelor's degree from Chestnut Hill College.